DETERMINED
FOR MORE

LIVING STONES

Cover Design by Jessica McNichol Creative
Interior Design by Milk & Honey Books, LLC

ISBN 13 TP: 979-8-9900241-0-6
ISBN 13 eBook: 979-8-9900241-1-3

DETERMINED FOR MORE

SHAWNA MEEK

TABLE OF CONTENTS

Part III: Trusting in the Purpose

INTRODUCTION

The Story Behind the Story

I have often felt alone in my marital journey.

Though I clung to the promises of God through the enduring pains, my hope was sometimes in the wrong things, such as the outcome I desired for my marriage, or my wish to see my husband do—or stop doing—something. I believe that many women are searching, as I was, for intimacy in their marriages and striving for deeper connection with their spouses, yet find themselves watching, with nowhere to turn for help, as that connection seems to be slipping away. Like so many others, I experienced profound confusion and was desperately seeking clarity.

There are many complexities to our struggles in marriage, and the most devastating are due to unspoken intimate betrayal, secret sexual deceptions, abusive and destructive behaviors, and attachment distress from childhood wounds. Where can wives go when they find themselves in these situations? It's not the sort of conversation you can have over the back fence with someone in your neighborhood. Even close friends don't know what to say. And many churches are neither equipped nor educated for these levels of destruction.

Too often, Christian answers are simplistic, dismissive, and barely scratch the surface: "pray more," "date your spouse," or "have more sex." Such comments leave struggling wives even more confused and devastated. What they face is something in need of far more than a simple fix. Desperate to understand why their marriages leave them feeling like they are dying inside; they cry out in the silence of their homes after the children go to bed. Hurt and lonely.

Wives need support from and connection with others who also have struggled during their marital journeys. They need someone to come alongside and authentically and honestly share coping strategies that will equip women to deal with destructive marriages. Most importantly, they need to know they are not alone.

My own struggle, hurt, and loneliness as I sought to deal with marital stress prompted me to begin mentoring others who were on the road I had already trekked. I sought professional training. That was the prelude to Living Stones and my career as a coach, mentor and consultant—someone who could walk with others, and most importantly, enable them to safely negotiate marital crises.

Quite a few times over the past years, I have been encouraged to share my story. Each casual comment piqued my interest enough to eventually put that idea on a bookshelf in my mind ... to consider later. Through the years, the thoughts whirling in my head have prompted me to speak our story aloud, mentor others, and lead couples' groups. But ... writing a book?

Unfortunately, writing, and public speaking have been some of my weakest areas, and the cause of much fear and trepidation. As a speaker, I fear not knowing what to say and the embarrassment of getting stumped while people stand there looking at me. Embarrassment and unknown expectations are the main activation points of fear for me.

As for writing? Deep inside, I had always dreamed of writing well, even eloquently. To be a fast reader was also something I deeply desired. But in my reality, English classes were always the source of my lower grades in school. Grammar, and vocabulary were particularly challenging. Though I haven't been officially diagnosed, I am confident that I have mild-to-moderate phonemic awareness dyslexia, so for many years, I couldn't enjoy reading.

Then, a few years back, when I shared an analogy that I had written in my journal, my husband, Kevin, joined the chorus: "You should write a book." I laughed under my breath, but I knew he wouldn't say that if he didn't believe it could happen. I remember answering, "Maybe someday. Who knows?" A week or so later, a good friend of mine sent me a book. "Wait until you open the package and see the similarities!" she said. The line on the cover read, *One Woman's Courageous Journey to Save Her Marriage*,[1] and the author had the same first name as I did. As I read the Foreword and then began the first chapter, I felt God prompting me subtly: *If she can write a book, so can you. You, too, have a story.*

Honestly, as I read her book, her story was at times eerily familiar. (It should come as no surprise that, today, I actively seek extra time to read!) One night, as I was talking with God, I said, "If this is what You want me to do, You're going to have to make this *really* clear, God." A bit of an audacious prayer, wasn't it?

The next morning, I shared my experience with Kevin. He asked, "How do you know God hasn't *already* made it clear?" I replied with a neutral "Hmmm," but I had to consider whether it was my own hesitation and doubt that had me bargaining with God the night before. In therapy, I had learned not to let my fears overtake me and how to be present in the moment. While my body might still react in fear, out of habit, the reactions within are a reasonable part of life.

I've come to a deeper understanding of what was missing in my marriage, and I've realized that God was asking me to write my story, then leave the outcome to Him. So, I began to write, and words came pouring out on the pages. Our story kept coming, word by word, paragraph by paragraph, until what you have in your hands was complete.

I've written our story for each one of you—a real and raw account of my journey from deep, dark valleys to the marital mountaintops—praying that God would give you the strength to be determined for more and trusting that you would never feel alone again.

PART I

Enduring Trials

"Dear brothers and sisters, whenever trouble comes your way, let it be an opportunity for joy. For when your faith is tested, your endurance has a chance to grow. So let it grow, for when your endurance is fully developed, you will be strong in character and ready for anything."
James 1:2-4

CHAPTER 1

Shattered Promises

Rollerblading on the strand of Newport Beach, California, on a Saturday afternoon was life. Getting up without an alarm, having a casual breakfast in my tiny apartment kitchen with my roommates, and making all my decisions the way I wanted were the rewards in my early twenties. Life was good. It was all I had envisioned. I'd left home at 18, gone to college for four years about an hour north of my parents' home all to land what I had envisioned as the ideal job at a boutique toy company that made all the trinkets for happy meals. But then I faced the question, *Where did I want my life to go from there?* Some college friends were getting married. Many other friends were still single.

I could live this single life, but I had to ask myself, *do I want that?* Such were the questions that ran through my young, naive mind. With only one previous relationship under my belt, there was a sense of innocence in me about a future marriage, with little to no thought of the calamity that could be.

As a child, I was independent, mostly confident, and fairly middle of the road about most things. From an early age, I spoke my opinion, even if that led to conflict. In my teen years, I used my voice often, even when there may have been consequences.

Sure, I believed that I had a few things I could certainly improve on, but overall, I wasn't "that bad." I made mostly good decisions, stayed low under the radar when it came to getting in trouble, and kept good friends. Some of my other classmates were certainly worse off than me. "Good" and "bad" were typically the only measures I had, and that's how I measured my life.

⌒

Kevin, now my husband of many years, grew up only a few miles from me though we didn't know each other until age 23. It was at a rugby tournament that we met; it was unique. My roommates and I were watching one of their boyfriends play on Veteran's Day. I noticed this cute guy in a uniform and hinted that my roommates should make their way in his direction. Kevin was working on standby as an EMT, awaiting any potential injuries. As we approached his ambulance, he asked if we wanted to check it out. Ambulances had always scared me, but I worked up the courage to spend a little time talking with him. He agreed to call, and later that evening, he did. There was some social unawareness and without him asking for me, my roommate ushered the phone to me. I was quite willing to talk. After that first hours-long call, similar conversations regularly followed.

He had already achieved many things in his young life: volunteering at a hospital in junior high, achieving Eagle Scout status at age 17, and taking honors classes. From that first call to our first date, I believed we could have a future together. I would get butterflies whenever we met, which felt good. But afterward, doubt always crept into my mind, a lingering uncertainty that I wasn't quite sure what to do with. Inside, he was less confident than his outward behavior indicated. He had some friends, but most of them were girls. He'd had a hard time connecting with kids his age, and I often wondered why.

Despite this, I proceeded. We moved quickly from dates (just us) to more public activities—events, and parties, and, after a short six weeks, we became involved with each other sexually. In our friend groups, that was the protocol: go out, tell someone you love them—or just like them—and have sex. Love and sex seemed to be strangely tied together for both of us. He didn't balk at this idea, nor did I. That was just the next step, and it is something we certainly don't brag about to our kids now.

With each passing month, we grew closer to talking about marriage and starting a family. We continued to spend a lot of time on the phone (a lost art for youthful relationships these days), and for the most part, we enjoyed each other's company. It was an odd sense of a friendship because we'd get along in conversation over the phone—our desires and thoughts would align—yet when it came to in-person moments, we would get snagged on communication and relationship issues that had, at first, seemed quite simple.

After merely a few weeks of hanging out together, I remember sharing a concern for an upcoming party we were going to be at with my friends. Together we had a few interactions with my friend group, and each time I would leave feeling as if Kevin was trying to get the attention, placing little value on the fact that these were my friends who I had known for years. When I was talking in this group of friends, he would interrupt me and try to fit into the conversation leaving me feeling awkward. I would look over at him with a glance as if to say, "Uh I was talking. Can I finish?" He wouldn't seem to notice. This brought feelings of self-doubt in my choice to be with someone who seemed to care more about how he came across versus how comfortable I felt. I wasn't sure if it was just arrogance or an insecurity he had. Could it be a social awkwardness that had nothing to do with me? Regardless, for that next upcoming party, I preemptively shared my concern from the last few times. He responded logically, yet it seemed he hadn't fully understood what I'd said. So I tried again to share my feelings. I sensed no compassion from him and felt confused why he didn't seem to want both of us to feel comfortable. That lack of compassion and understanding led to conflict. It was as if we were speaking different languages, and I tried hard to help him understand my heart.

Thereafter, we cycled through the same types of arguments at levels of conflict so high resolution was often difficult. Looking back at those early months, I now realize how important being heard was to me and what a struggle "hearing" me was for him.

Due to our mutually high value on family and children, however, we continued to talk about the future of our relationship despite these snags. Honestly? I wanted kids even more than a marriage, and he wanted what seemed to be the right next thing: to be with someone forever.

Looking back, marriage conversations moved fast for us in our early 20s, but we fell into it anyway. When we excitedly bought a condo together, that opened the door to what we believed was the next clear step: talking about the possibility of a wedding. We even discussed the ring. But all in the future tense. No need to be in a hurry. So, I thought. But one typical weeknight after work, we had planned to have dinner together, and I had my head in the fridge when he abruptly stopped me: "I can't wait anymore. This is burning a hole in my pocket," he said. "Will you marry me?" His emotional affect was relatively flat. There was limited inflection in his voice and his expression resembled happiness but not the level of excitement and warmth I would have anticipated when he proposed. The words he used sounded more like he was uncomfortable with the waiting, focused on the results instead of connection. You can imagine my face. *What? Was this a joke?* He didn't just propose now, did he? Confusion whirled in my head before I had a chance to think of a reply. I don't remember what my next words were, but I think I said something like, "Are you serious?" He surely was. So, I answered. I said, "Yes."

We were wed 11 months after the proposal on October 18, 1997. It was beautiful, and though I didn't practice all the foundations of the Catholic faith, we were married in a Catholic church as friends and family stood by our sides. Although my nerves and doubts were still present, as evidenced in the old VHS recording we watched again recently, we loved each other. We loved what we could have together: a future of promise. That was clear, despite our somewhat rocky moments in courtship.

A spunky Labrador Retriever came six months later, followed by a new house, six months after that. All the pieces seemed to be falling into place to complete the plan of what was supposed to be, including the part I had always imagined, the part for which I had longed: being a mom. Indeed, our first baby, a boy, Connor James, was born in December 1999 nine months after we moved into our house. We loved being parents. We loved Connor deeply, and though everything wasn't completely jovial all the time, he seemed to bring us happiness that outweighed the struggle.

But struggle we did. Our communication issues continued. But, I reasoned, wouldn't any new marriage, with a new house, a new dog, and a new baby certainly have some problems? Shortly after Connor was born, however, we decided counseling was appropriate. I remember walking into our first counseling session that summer in 2000 feeling some shame that we needed this, especially so soon, but I certainly welcomed the possibility that we might find some sort of relief. We went every week, but what followed our sessions was tumultuous. It was almost as if the pressure of counseling was making things harder. It seemed that our attempts to repair the hurt and wounds of only a few years together only exaggerated the conflict. I never enjoyed conflict but appreciated its value. I could picture the long-term gains, but Kevin became increasingly overwhelmed the more we opened up in our conversations.

It became evident that we needed the help, and I was hopeful that we could eventually develop the skills to talk and relate better with one another. I realized, later, that when you wait to resolve issues that existed before you married, the foundation of the newly identified roles as husband and wife can be seriously disrupted. In our case, the dance that would later become so very destructive had long ago begun to take form: I had become the *pursuer*, and he, the *withdrawer*.[1]

I would move toward him relationally, but the closer I came, the farther he would pull away. It seemed so unnatural to me. I wanted to be close. He *said* he wanted to be close, but we couldn't make it happen. There were times our conversation would get heated, and instead of trying to see each other's perspectives, we would get louder and end with him leaving the house. Sometimes, I would even go after him, nearly chasing him down our long street. I just wanted him to open up to me so I could better understand what just happened, but running from things was what he had learned to do well. I had perfected persistently chasing after things, and I could feel him pulling farther away as time went on. In session, each passing week, I would think that, maybe, we were getting somewhere. I believed we could work this out. But after the session, our pursuit/withdrawal again became a volatile combination.

I wanted no more than to raise our son in a loving home with two parents who got along for the most part and could equally share that love with him. He was a sweet baby, smiling early on, seemingly unfazed by our early arguments. Thankfully, we mostly didn't argue much around him.

CHAPTER 2

Hit by a Train

One morning, on an average day a few months after our counseling began, Kevin headed off to work and I kissed him goodbye, as usual. I was working very part-time at that point, so I was home with Connor. He was at my very favorite part of the baby stage: sitting up, giggling, amused by my very presence, rocking back and forth on all fours—ready to be on the move. It was a lazy day ahead with Connor still asleep in his crib. I dozed off to sleep again with plans for us to join a moms' group function or just take a stroll around the block in our little neighborhood later on. After about an hour or so, to my surprise, Kevin came home and walked back into the bedroom, asking if we could talk.

Though it was 24 years ago, my stomach still churns a bit with memories of that morning. Something was wrong. I had never seen Kevin look quite this distressed and upset. I don't remember his exact words, having not yet even sat up, but they hit me like a freight train. There was no mistaking his meaning: He was leaving. He wanted a divorce. He said he couldn't be a husband anymore. He wasn't equipped for it, and that was it. His mind was made up.

I was in complete disbelief and felt shocked like never before. How could this be? In *my* mind, we had been making progress. We had a future ahead of us. What about our sweet eight-month-old baby, who was still asleep in the new little nursery with light blue walls and stars all around?

———

Looking back, I had the difficult task of letting my mind and body take in what he was saying. I remember the room and where I was lying, but nothing else. It was as if the whole world had stopped. It was too big to handle in those initial moments. He seemed so certain. *He couldn't do this.* Those words still stand out clearly in my memory. I'm guessing he must have said more during the hour we spoke but I don't recall it. After the discussion, he said he was going to talk with our counselor and then take a walk on the beach. He was in a dark place and offered me no comfort. The despair and our collective pain were overwhelming.

He never blamed me, however, nor made it about me. I found this so odd. I had heard of similar situations before, in which spouses would place the blame somewhere else, so they didn't have to take it all on. But Kevin actually blamed himself and his inadequacies. It truly never seemed to be about me as a person or as a spouse, and looking back, I can see that his mind and nervous system were terribly overloaded. But then, in my distress, I wondered why the marriage had to go? Was it all the changes we had in our life? Why did he commit to marriage if he couldn't handle it? Why was he having such extreme reactions?

Without options and lacking anyone with whom to share our struggles, I did what I thought was best. I couldn't stay in that house that day and look around at all we had started in our short two-and-a-half years of marriage, so I moved back in with my parents. Kevin's words to me came as a complete shock to my family and close friends as well. They were as heartbroken as I was.

I'm not sure how I made it through the shock of those early days. I even struggled to feed our baby, despite reminders from others. Day after day, I pursued: Kevin and I would talk. I hoped he would change his mind. I would ask questions, plead, and remind him of the promises he made to us, and cry with him as he stayed on the phone, listening. Gradually, but ultimately, he withdrew. With each day and week came more certainty that he was moving forward with divorce. He had talked to our counselor, and I'm guessing the counselor couldn't convince him otherwise either. I remember not fully trusting that the counselor believed in commitment to marriage the way I did, but he was the first counselor I had known. Since we'd started with him just six months prior, I had not thought, even for a moment, this would be the course our marriage would take.

This was also my introduction to grief, and it felt awful. I had lost grandparents before this and had some sad moments and shed some tears, but this was on a completely different level—one I had never imagined possible. There were sleepless nights, rocking my baby with tears streaming down my face, and nursing him, only to realize much later I was passing on the stress hormones through my breast milk. I never wanted this, and yet my appeal for more was not heard. I even prayed to God, who I vaguely felt was near. I began to realize I needed to relinquish control of my marriage. I needed to build a resilience for which I never knew I had the capacity.

————————

It wasn't long before divorce papers were filed with the state of California that November. In California, you had to wait a full year from the date of separation; our divorce would be final in August 2001.

I had so many difficult mornings, waking up alone, and days walking around in a daze. At night, I lost sleep, but somehow, I knew I would be okay. I was desperately sad that I couldn't have any more children with him. I loved how we both lit up being parents together. I never wanted my kids to be far apart in age, and who knew, now, if I would ever even *want* to get married again? At this point, it was a big *NO!*

That year, we went through mediation to finalize the divorce versus spending time and money on attorneys. We were cordial. He didn't fight me about much, and agreed to what I thought were fair requests on my part.

CHAPTER 3

Setting Boundaries, Moving On

With the divorce underway, I began a new chapter of life. Kevin stayed in our first home until it sold as I certainly didn't want to be there to deal with all that. I knew staying at my parents' house forever wasn't ideal, either, so I bought myself a small, detached townhouse, and, after the sale of the house we'd shared, Kevin bought and moved into a condo. We were only a few miles apart, so it was relatively easy to share custody.

I had 80 percent custody of Connor, and Kevin and I worked out the time-sharing details together well. We would meet every month to go over anything related to Connor. We had an agenda, and we followed it. It's as if the cognitive and emotional demands were lighter for him—though he lost his family—but connection was easier for him as simply parents. I think Connor truly benefited from that amicable arrangement, despite his little life being disrupted so early. That early trauma and our times of emotional unavailability are sad for me to look back on. It wasn't supposed to be that way, and I believed it didn't have to be that way.

At times, however, Kevin wanted to be a part of our lives as if nothing had changed. Our first Halloween apart, Kevin was stuck in traffic and nearly missed going around trick-or-treating with Connor in his stroller. I had invited him because we always agreed to put Connor's needs first. He was devastated to be late, nearly in tears. I never really hated Kevin for what he had done; I honestly felt more pity and sadness. Despite my compassion for him that night, I remember thinking, "This is a natural consequence of your decision." I wondered if he felt that same weight of consequence, yet those weren't things we talked about anymore. I certainly also had anger and felt the weight of those consequences, but these moments were part of the grieving process for me.

I learned that the grieving process has six stages: shock, denial, bargaining, anger, sadness, and acceptance. I experienced sadness for a while, bouncing back to the earlier stages and every so often tipping into acceptance. It was a process, and I found great comfort in taking all the time I needed.

I had begun to see a new individual counselor soon after Kevin left. I had within me a relentless drive and the moxie necessary to heal and learn about myself and others. Sessions could be grueling, and I wouldn't even look at anyone as I quickly left the office. Most days, I had puffy eyes and my makeup rubbed off, thanks to all the tissues. This was my time, though, with my therapist. I found it so healing to work through each piece I needed to. It helped me so much to learn how to forgive, how to move forward, and how not to be stuck forever in the place I was in. Certainly, the fate of my marriage was determined by Kevin's decision, but that decision didn't have to determine the rest of my life. I could move forward. I could have hope for my future. I was soon willing to see what was ahead of me. That resilience I had begun to build within me increased.

I did miss Kevin, despite the cruddy decision he had made, and I missed the life I thought we would have. Through the confusing emotions, I had to try on some new boundaries. Boundaries came naturally in some areas of my life, but I didn't understand them in this realm. I bought books on single parenting. Some would talk about boundaries and how not to slip back into old patterns with an ex. Despite my emotional and physical desires at times, I wanted to make sure that my expectations were clear to Kevin, since clear structure and rules had already helped us elsewhere:

- No calling me to share your life.
- No physical touch.
- No crossing over into my life with questions.
- No long conversations about anything other than Connor.

Life without these boundaries was too confusing for me. Allowing him to cross them would send me backward, and I didn't want to go backward. I had always been someone who could receive tough news, work through it, and do my best to move forward. In my mind, this situation wouldn't look much different.

Connor didn't seem to notice all of this. He was still very young, and I don't ever recall him asking many questions, like, "Why do I have two houses?" He had lived in *five* homes by the time he was two years old. That broke my heart, and I tried to make it as simple for him as possible. My sweet boy and I moved into our little two-bedroom house in August 2001, around the time the divorce was finalized. This was a space for me to heal and the first time I was on my own with Connor. We made it ours. He seemed comfortable and typically went to his dad's house every other weekend and a couple of nights a week. I had a much tougher time than Connor did with the weekends apart, and though I was moving on, I remember rocking him night after night and praying over his little heart, hoping God would spare him the consequences of all this pain and destruction. Still, we had established our new routine, and we were going to be alright. A faith had been forged in the fire of this affliction as I accepted our circumstances and fought to make the best of them.

CHAPTER 4

In God's Presence

"From there, you will search again for the Lord your God. And if you search for Him with all your heart and soul, you will find him," Deuteronomy 4:29.

I had known about God, but I hadn't known the presence and loving care of the divine God. Yet He felt close during this treacherous time in my life. I wondered what more there was that I was missing. Being married in a Catholic church was mainly because Kevin had chosen this denomination a few years prior to our marriage. He had been searching for religion and for something or someone to keep his course straight. I attended a Catholic church a few times during our marriage, and after our marriage dissolved, I enrolled in a divorce recovery class there that was a beautiful lifeline.

There is a part of me that has been longing since I was little—I will share about it in more detail much later in this book—that keeps searching for vulnerable safe places to be known and relate to others in similar situations. I knew I needed this support even though I had streams of tears that first evening. The class gave me hope that I was going to heal and would come out whole from this situation with the eternal love of God. I had chosen not to take the classes necessary to convert to Catholicism prior to our wedding, but I did believe that God was who He said He was. I just couldn't understand God in the way He was presented, and so I waited. I came to believe wholeheartedly that God was grieving the loss of our marriage and our family. This hadn't been His plan or His doing at all.

Growing up, we dabbled in church but were never consistent church-goers. I was a strong-willed, independent young girl—maybe too independent. I knew, or at least believed I knew, what was best for my life. I didn't have a Higher Power that guided me. It was more accurate to say that I depended on my conscience, my will, and the fear of doing something extreme that kept me in check. This was how I experienced "the fear of God."

After the divorce, it was my opportunity to discover my beliefs and exercise my choice to see Who this God really was. I began attending another church, this time a non-denominational Christian church close to where I bought my new home. I was reaching for connection and understanding, so it made sense to me. They worshipped the same Father, Son, and Holy Spirit—that didn't change—yet I found a relationship with Jesus there. I felt free to discover the depths of a friendship with Jesus, who saw all of me. I wanted this connection where human connection had failed, and I deeply desired to know more about this God of the Universe they were talking about.

Little by little, I learned. I stepped out and took a class to discover what it meant to be a believer in Jesus. I made the decision one weekend in church to accept Jesus as my personal

Savior. I wanted to follow Him. I wanted to have Him guide my life. I wanted to turn over my life and give up doing things on my own. Though I was making it day to day, going my way alone was not working well, and I admitted that I had to stop trying to be so independent. It was a perfectly simple and right decision for me. Admittedly, I think I "decided" at least two more times, when the pastor led the prayer of commitment, just to be sure. Maybe that was a clue to my self-doubt. Allowing Jesus to come into my life and be a power greater than myself was a process, but I haven't thought twice about my decision to do so since then. Through the grueling days ahead, He became my source of strength even amidst the struggle and angst with Him.

I would like to just pause my story for a minute here and share the heartache that comes for me when I hear stories of human relationships, religions, institutions, and sources of authority that encourage others to accept Jesus using condemnation, guilt and shame. I didn't have that in my story, but I would be remiss not to say *I hate that for you* if this is a part of your story. I take a deep breath and relax my shoulders as I write this because I feel angered by the injury this may have caused you. I'm so sorry. This is not the Jesus I have met, and I understand it may take time to untangle the truth of who He is from the lie you may have heard. You deserve to have spaces and people in your life to explore who Jesus is to you and what He wants you to know about His care and adoration of you, too.

I had a lot of questions about my new faith. There was so much to learn, and the Bible felt intimidating to me. But I opened it and started in from the beginning. I wish I had known then what I know now: starting with the book of Matthew in the Gospels could have been a better option for newbies like me. That knowledge would have saved me from starting with Genesis and stopping in Exodus multiple times over the first few years. Most of my friends hadn't grown up in church, so I didn't have many people to whom I felt close enough to ask questions.

Despite that slow start, I kept coming back to church and did meet some people who knew a bit more than me. Kevin began to come from time to time with Connor, too, so it was something we could briefly talk about. But I made sure to keep the boundaries that I was learning about in place, so we didn't get into tricky territory.

CHAPTER 5

That Letter

It had been about a year and a half since Kevin walked out. I wasn't interested in dating yet, but I did decide to join the young-adult singles group at church. It gave me a chance to connect with others who were in the same or similar situations and was a good way to get my feet wet in my new church life. Going to the group's events, however, was awkward. I felt like a teenager walking into a school dance, knowing full well I didn't have any rhythm.

At these events, most people seemed to have a right relationship with God and a reason for being there, but occasionally, I would notice that guy who was looking for a fresh date. I wasn't interested and was even repelled by the idea early on. Slowly, however, I began to consider whether I would even date again. Our group went on outings with our kids: hikes, picnics, events at the church. It was a good step for me to reenter the world beyond my job and the friends I had known for years. Above all, I wanted to be sure I would follow God and have a relationship with Jesus. I didn't know if marriage was even a possibility again. Some days, I was interested, but on other days, thinking about going through all that again made me want to throw up. I questioned whether I could judge another's character and commitment, so the Lord felt like a safe bet for my next season of courtship.

Nevertheless, I did think about what it might be like to date again. Then I would shy away from the thought. I would come back to Jesus and be in prayer, asking Him to guide my steps. The pain of even considering dating was immense at times. I continued to grieve the losses: That I might have no other children and that Connor might not have siblings to grow up with. In fact, there were a lot of losses to count, so far, and I wanted to be cautious in my steps.

As Connor approached the age of three, and after much time and prayer, I decided that I would be open to dating in the summer of 2002. I had returned to work full time out of necessity, and I'd actually found a dating service that supported professionals, long before such things were readily available online. I don't know if it still exists today, but this service seemed less scary because dating prospects were interviewed and then screened to a certain level. Despite the ridiculous amount of money I spent on this vetting process, it felt like the right next step. What could I lose?

Kevin and I had agreed that Connor was not to be around anyone either of us dated until the other had been informed. I remember reading that somewhere and it was a boundary I could hold on to, for some semblance of control. This felt like a safe approach and allowed me to bring my values into the screening process. It was a much different experience than that typical of my previously random meetings with new people at rugby games, parties or, not so many years earlier, local bars.

Thankfully, I had grown up and matured some since my earlier crazy days of partying with friends and hoping to find someone I wanted to spend the rest of my life with. Dating in this new fashion felt sophisticated. But then the service set me up on a few dates, and none of them amounted to much. I wasn't too interested, and I'm not sure any of the guys were, either.

Creating chemistry and flirting were not my strong suits. I could put myself together nicely but never really learned how to put out that cute, carefree vibe that I thought most guys were looking for. Even though I had developed a certain degree of self-confidence, dating was, sometimes, just crazy awkward.

There was, however, one guy that I specifically remember talking to more consistently than the others. He was a friend of someone I knew, so the fancy dating service hadn't been necessary in that case. He treated me well, took me to a nice restaurant on the beach, and then proceeded at one point on that first date to tell me he smoked marijuana nearly every day. *What?* I remember thinking that, while I did have my party days, this was a bit extreme for my liking, especially now that I was a mom. The daily use was a deal breaker.

There was one other guy I went on a few dates with. I felt like he was a bit more into me than I was into him, for once. He was a believer in Jesus, generous, and compassionate, and even showed some signs of empathy—a new experience for me from a man in my life. I had the feeling that I was not quite ready to move forward with him. I found myself coming back to God for many conversations about my lack of interest. The very things I craved—being pursued, receiving empathy, having interest in me, being treated well—were not drawing me closer to him. I did not have a physical connection to him. That was discouraging, but I knew it was the best decision. If God already had plans for me laid out, and He had a promising future for my life, then I could make a choice to trust Him. One of my favorite Scriptures of that time was, *"The truth is that you will be in Babylon for seventy years. But then I will come and do for you all the good things I have promised, and I will bring you home again. 'For I know the plans I have for you,' says the Lord. 'They are plans for good and not for disaster, to give you a future and a hope,'"* Jeremiah *29:10-11.* I just needed to sit back and let it unfold. I was trying my best to be patient in the waiting, which felt so much more peaceful.

One evening in late 2002, I had literally just sat back on my couch, when Kevin arrived to drop off Connor for the night. We still had our stellar co-parenting plan and had tried to make it as seamless for Connor as possible (If there was ever an award for rock star co-parents, I truly think we would have received it). After he put Connor to bed and Kevin said goodbye to him, he walked back downstairs, then handed me a letter, asking me to read it after he left. I'm sure my face had a quite contorted look on it as he abruptly walked out. My hands began to tremble as I opened the letter. My heart started beating faster, my stomach tightened, and my palms began to sweat.

It was over a page of Kevin's tiny handwritten print, and the gist of it was this: "I now realize how much I have put you through. I am terribly sorry, and I never wanted to hurt you. I have done my own counseling and work on myself, and I believe I have made a mistake. Will you consider dating again?" Shock and disbelief came flooding in. My mind raced. *What was I reading? How did I not see this coming? Was he serious? He'd delivered a marriage proposal when my head was buried in the fridge, and now this? Why had this taken so long? What the heck?!*

The cry from my heart was, "Of course, I want my family back together again," but my rational brain wanted to say, "Of course not! You lost that chance. Leave me alone and don't confuse me now." I was deeply divided as I sat there on the second cushion of my sage green sectional. My eyes blankly stared at that piece of paper and then abruptly shifted, turning to the front door just steps away that he had exited. That pattern repeated as I continued to soak in what had just occurred. It baffled me. I hadn't seen the divorce coming, and I hadn't seen this coming, either. It was nearly two-and-a-half years since he'd announced his decision to leave me, and in that time, he had not once wavered. I knew he had been to counseling, but we also had agreed that we would not talk about the deep issues between us so as to not get too entangled with our lives. I had seen some changes, but truly, I wasn't the best judge of who he was, clearly.

No one in particular stood out in my dating life at that moment, so I had planned to move on. I was thinking of a future for Connor and myself and would consider who I dated through that filter. Kevin's letter arrived mere days before I was to attend, for a second time, an annual single-parents retreat in the mountains. It was going to be a long weekend, but now I knew I needed that time away more than ever.

In my newfound relationship with God, I had begun to trust that He knew what He was doing or, certainly, knew what was happening. I was so grateful not to have to make a decision about Kevin's request alone or with only my friends and family, who were understandably biased. I don't recall telling anyone about the letter before I left for the retreat. I just packed it in my bag and headed up the mountain.

———————

Many of my free moments at the retreat were spent sitting on a large rock, praying for clarity and asking for direction. *What good could come of dating my ex-husband? Why all the heartache only to come back to this place? And what about Connor? Oh God, really what are you doing? I'm not sure. Are you trustworthy? Why? Why now?*

At first, the questions were non-stop. I tried my best to rest in the place of not knowing all the answers immediately, but the absence of clear resolution was quite anxiety-provoking. I chose, despite my fear-filled feelings, to trust in and hope for a plan God may have in all this. Then—I remember that one particular moment, sitting on that rock—God brought peace over me that, quite honestly, I couldn't understand. I, too, needed to hear Paul's reminder to the church of Philippi:

"Don't worry about anything; instead, pray about everything. Tell God what you need and thank Him for all He has done. If you do this, you will experience God's peace, which is far more wonderful than the human mind can understand. His peace will guard your hearts and minds as you live in Christ Jesus," *Philippians 4:6-7.*

It wasn't an audible answer. It wasn't the loud Voice that I so desperately wanted to hear. It was, instead, a quiet stillness that came over me as I sat and reflected: Dating Kevin again *didn't* mean I was going to remarry him. It was just a date. And if I didn't date him, I knew I would always wonder what God's intention in all of this had been. Maybe He was giving me back a gift, but I wasn't sure I was ready to receive it. There was a lot on the line. In my heart, I'd found some incredible healing, and forgiveness truly had been given to Kevin years before, by the Lord's grace. Would dating Kevin undo all that God had done? The risk was great, but I realized that the reward could be greater. I'd become willing to see what God had for me and for us. From my perspective, Kevin really was walking in a much more genuine way with himself now. He'd said there were parts of his scarred heart that he hadn't known how to show me before because of his fear of not being good enough and not valuing himself. He expressed a desire to let me experience parts of him that were hidden even from himself. He was willing to hear my experience through the divorce and really sit with me and listen.

I sensed a level of care for me I didn't know he had. The fruit of his therapy work was showing. So, I chose to see the changes and his deep journey of growth during our time apart. I felt a calm reassurance, hearing things I longed to hear before, such as "you deserve a committed husband, one that won't leave you again." He wanted to walk the road I had originally wanted to walk and uphold the commitments we had made in our vows. There was a newness in him, and I was grateful to see it. He was more attentive toward me and seemed open to discussing all the processes he had gone through. He committed to never again leave me. He committed to re-connecting slowly in the right and honorable way. I chose to receive that promise of absolutes.

So, I agree to go on a date.

CHAPTER 6

Dating Him Once More

Our second first date, much sweeter than the last, came in November 2002. The care and concern for my heart were evident where it had only mildly been there before. There were triggers along the way, for sure, but there was also healing as we discussed things together and grieved what we had walked through. He shared more truthfully than he ever had before. I was open to dating him again to see how things progressed.

Honesty, however, was still a struggle for him in some ways. That struggle showed itself a few months into dating. One of my biggest desires in starting our life together again was to have more children. He said he had the same desire. We discussed trying to conceive quickly if we remarried, because the age gap between the kids was already going to be bigger than we wanted.

Not wanting to disappoint me, he withheld the fact that, while we were apart, he'd had a vasectomy. It had been three months since the letter he'd written, and many dates and phone calls had followed, allowing us access to deeper parts of each other's hearts again. Then, the admission. For this conversation, I sat at my four-chaired kitchen table on the phone with him in the little house that had so much meaning and was free from deception and mistruths until this moment. The sink in my stomach. The yellow flag waving in front of my face which only heeded temporary caution.

I sat there stunned with confusion on my face—which he couldn't see through the phone—and I asked point blank, "Why didn't you tell me sooner?" I could feel my blood pumping faster and my heart rate increasing. He began to apologize while down-playing his reasons. A flash moment of *who is this guy?* raced through my mind. He said that he had planned to tell me. *Ya, when?* He said he knew it was important to me to have more kids and things were going well with us. He was going to tell me. *As if this wasn't important for me to know much sooner! Did he even think of me? Was he trying to spin the story to make himself look better? Was this a moment of fear?*

I was left wondering what to do with this covert deception. He was willing to have the vasectomy reversed even before we remarried, so that was the agreed-upon plan. It wasn't a complete deal breaker for me, but certainly, it was a choice he made that could have severe consequences if the reversal didn't take. But I also made a choice, the consequence of which could also be severe: Though the deception caused a bit of trust to be lost again, and the new foundation we were building fractured some, I felt it was repairable. I have often wondered through the years why I so quickly thought it was repairable and why he wasn't thinking about me in withholding that information. He was sorry but was more concerned about making it better so we could move forward. And that distracted me.

We dated for six months while still living in California, and when away at a couple's retreat, he gave me a redemptive marriage proposal—very different from the first—in a hot air balloon as the sun rose over the Arizona desert. We were remarried August 18, 2003, almost three years to the day after he had walked out: We chose a small ceremony in Hawaii with my immediate family and made a vacation out of it. Connor was even a part of the wedding. Our family was back together again, and my heart was full, and I was so very grateful for the restoration God had allowed in our hearts and our lives.

After returning from the wedding, we received the news that the vasectomy reversal had taken, and we conceived our second child, another baby boy, two months later. His conception was a true gift in this time of joy and transition. We found a new house together—number six for Connor—and I quit my job to stay home with Tyler Joseph, who was born in July 2004, as Connor was finishing up preschool.

Tyler's happy disposition was exactly what my heart needed, what our family needed. The boys had each other now. They adored each other even with the many years between them. My fears of not having more than one child were gone.

It wasn't long before we made another major life choice. You would have thought we would have learned by now that transitions and changes caused us harm and were especially challenging for Kevin. Regardless, six months later, I prayerfully chose to have an elective double mastectomy. My immediate family has an extremely high risk of certain types of cancer, and I had an 89 percent chance of getting breast cancer in my lifetime and somewhere around a 50 percent chance by the time

I was in my forties. After meeting with a genetic counselor in 2003, shortly before we remarried, it was determined that I had the gene mutation of BRCA 1 and had options to reduce my risk, which led to my decision to have the surgery. I felt confident in this decision and thankful I had surgical options to help me have the best chance of being able to care for my precious children throughout their childhoods. I had a lot of support from family and friends because this was major surgery especially while caring for a newborn. And Kevin was there each step of the way. He really showed up. He stayed with me in the hospital, changed my bandages, changed baby diapers at home. This was his sweet spot, and there were a lot of moving pieces.

Not to anyone's surprise, Kevin began nursing school just after Tyler was born and a few months before my surgery. Another change, indeed. He had always wanted to be a nurse. He hadn't made that choice previously for a variety of reasons. One—I'm not proud to say—was my attitude about it— along the lines of "Guys aren't supposed to be nurses." I had belittled and controlled him with such comments, and it was an ugly-hearted judgment that had tremendously influenced his self-esteem, exacerbating his feelings of defeat and lack of confidence in himself as a husband.

Another reason was my concern about Kevin working in a field where his co-workers would be primarily females. I thought that was a dangerous career choice for any male. Temptation could be high, and I'd already had my concerns over his mostly female friendships in the early days of our relationship. I felt fear deep within and didn't know how to express or honor my concerns, since there wasn't evidence of anything going awry.

But this time around, I was truly in full support during the application process. I trusted his commitment and was proud that he was pursuing a career he wanted. I had abandoned my silly bias, and I gave him the support he needed.

Halfway through his time in nursing school, however, my immediate family began to seriously discuss a move from California to somewhere with less-expensive housing prices. We had long considered such a move as well, and I believed I needed to have my extended family close by or life would be too hard for me. Kevin expressed he was alright with moving, so my parents, my brother and his wife, and my little family of four rallied together and decided on Arizona.

After many trips east on the I-10 freeway, we found a house under construction six hours away in a locale where Kevin was able to secure a job that would be waiting for him, upon graduation, in a local Trauma ICU. We sold our house in California and made the move in the dead of the summer heat. I'm not sure why anyone moves to Arizona in the summer, but such was our timing.

We soon settled into our home, but it took many years for me to find roots. California was all I had known, and, though my family was with us, I wanted to find connection with new friends. Church, of course, had become important to us, so we tried a few churches and quickly landed at our home church. I can say with all certainty that we would not be where we are today without this gift to us.

We still planned on growing our family. But before leaving California, Kevin went back for a follow-up appointment, and we found out that scar tissue from the vasectomy reversal had built up. He would need another surgery, but this time the odds of success were low. Sadly, Kevin had elected a vasectomy while we were apart because he wanted nothing to compromise his effort to be the best possible dad to Connor and feared that children from another relationship might get in the way. His decision making was quite black and white—like the divorce— and focused on short-term solutions. Despite the pain his decision was falling upon our renewed relationship, Kevin's dedication and commitment to his boy brought me pride.

As we established things in Arizona and Kevin began his nursing career, his second surgery beat the odds! We became pregnant with a baby girl. Everyone was overjoyed. This second, sweet miracle baby from two vasectomy reversals was likely the completion of our family, so we thought. The boys wanted a sister. We spent nights praying together for her and planned a scavenger hunt gender reveal around our neighborhood. We welcomed Katelyn Grace in February 2007, and the ensuing years brought much joy, laughter, and chaos to our family of five as Kevin worked full-time as a nurse, and I was able to stay home with the kids.

It soon became time to consider another preventative surgery. Nine months after Katelyn joined our family, I chose to have my ovaries, uterus, and fallopian tubes removed to eliminate further risk of cancer. As I made this challenging decision about my health for the sake of my longevity with them, I was also experiencing growing concern within me about our marriage. Kevin had been more present early on after our remarriage, but I had this sense of danger, as if Kevin were leaving and never coming back. My breath increased to fill my lungs with the needed oxygen. The tension in the back of my neck would alert me that my adrenals were on high alert.

These triggers would come on suddenly—I had no say in the matter—while I was looking at my young children playing, enjoying a moment alone in the shower, or simply washing dishes. It was a cruel sense of distress. But I would willfully remind myself, "Your story is different now."

CHAPTER 7

Hit by a Train Again

I had built endurance through the divorce and remarriage, and I was proud of my newly established trust in God, my main source of strength. Life now felt somewhat normal. I'd found some roots in our new neighborhood and church. The kids were involved in age-appropriate activities, and I loved being a mom. While motherhood was such an enjoyable part of my life, I also desperately wanted a deeper connection with my husband. We weren't completely distant, but things were getting rough again. Kevin worked at a different hospital now and was taking overtime shifts. He became increasingly emotionally distant, and I couldn't quite figure it out, despite trying. I pursued; he withdrew. I used all my old strategies to get him to open up: buying devotionals to do together at night, setting a time on the calendar to talk, asking him his feelings, and if he didn't know, giving him multiple-choice answers. Nothing quite worked, and I became convinced something was off.

In May 2009, as Kevin prepared to leave the next morning for the annual men's retreat at church, I knew something was terribly wrong—broken. Our arguments were never over the big stuff, such as finances and parenting. They always involved little issues blowing up into huge ones. Our issues almost always were about emotion and connection. Conflict usually started with something sounding much like this: "I felt caught off guard & embarrassed when we were with our friends last night and we were laughing, and then all of a sudden, I was the butt of your joke. I looked over to you and again, you didn't even notice what you were doing. I have no idea why that was funny to you and what made you share that. I don't want to put myself in those situations. I feel worse when I go with you and you do that. I would prefer to be alone with my friends." And instead of him trying to hear me and my concern, it would be met with something like, "I was just kidding. Didn't think that would be such a big issue for you. Here we go again." What was a seemingly small hurt I was trying to share with him got bigger really quick with the logical reply, and narrow-minded focus. We missed each other often like this, and what seemed to be a desire for repair would end up leaving things in further disrepair.

So much seemed hidden under the surface. Consistent misinterpretation, misunderstanding and misjudgment led to grueling and explosive conversations. One evening, a bomb went off. I don't remember the topic we fought about, but I remember the explosion. The emotional deprivation had been building, and with each seemingly small concern I had, he shut me down quickly. I was done, just done with this neglectful dance. I reacted. We both raised our voices and said some mean words. I said critical things to him about his lack of care for me while he could care for his patients, work, and the children so well. He got right in my face, so I pushed him with both hands in the chest.

He stormed out of the bedroom. I shouted from the top of the stairs, which elicited a livid revisit in the bedroom, a few more choice words, and Kevin slamming the bedroom door behind him and sleeping on the couch that night. We didn't speak again before he left for the retreat the next day.

The retreat topic was how to have a relationship with Jesus instead of simply practicing a religion. Kevin had known how to do religion well. Though a relationship with Christ was foreign to him, it all clicked that weekend. He was brought to tears by the words from the guest speaker and later shared with me the impact that message had on him. God had truly spoken to him about releasing his need to perform and to stop striving to make himself better, more worthy, more significant. He came home visibly refreshed, and we were somewhat back on track after our horrendous fight.

The last week of school before summer, and only a week after the retreat, we came home after going out to eat. Kevin went up to our bed around the same time we put the kids down, so I stayed up to get some things done on the computer in our nook in the kitchen. Those quiet evenings were the time when I would often get to wrap up things I was working on, so this night was routine for me. As I was sitting there thinking about what I was going to do next, there was a buzz in the cabinet above my head. It was the cabinet that held our keys, wallets, and phones. I opened it and realized Kevin's phone was buzzing. He had forgotten to take it up with him before bed. I rarely looked at his phone, but this time, I did.

My heart beats a little faster, even as I type these words today. There was a text on his phone from someone I didn't know. It said, "Haven't seen you in a while, we should go to lunch sometime." Something inside me dropped. I stared at the text for a moment that felt more like five minutes. With trembling legs, I walked upstairs, leaving no room for wandering thoughts. I woke Kevin and asked who it was and what it was about. He was groggy but woke up enough to answer: "Oh, it's just someone from work."

It probably seemed to him like this dismissive and vague response would get me to stop asking questions. But a nagging persistence kept me pressing, and nothing he said was sufficient. I remember saying, "That doesn't make sense. Why wouldn't you have told me if this was just a friend? That breaks my trust. I need to know everything."

At this point, I began to cry and shook inside, not even realizing the severity of the issue. Trust had been broken, and the feelings were strong. I know now that the Holy Spirit allowed me to see what I saw in that very rare moment, and He was guiding me through each minute of that night. It's as if he were saying directly to me: *"For everything that is hidden or secret will eventually be brought to light and made plain to all,"* Luke 8:17. Though I desperately feared what I might discover, I held tight to the conviction that something just wasn't right. At the time, sheer determination drove my pleas for answers. I found myself pacing in the room and not knowing where to turn. I needed to know, yet I wasn't going to stay there standing next to the bed. I went to my closet to cry, instead. It felt safest there. It was farther away from the kids' room, and I had no idea what was to come. Little did I know it was the best shelter I had to let my shattered heart fall to pieces. I wasn't sure what was happening, but I felt like I had been hit by a train for the second time.

Moments later, Kevin got up and followed me into the closet. I remember uttering the words again, "Tell me everything. I need to know everything." I believed deep down that something was terribly wrong, but there had only been one specific time that I even had an inkling of suspicion that he could be unfaithful in our marriage. Although my own doubt was a faithful friend of mine, this was different. There was a trusting in myself and courage that felt quite supernatural. I clung to what I could from the conversation and tried to get the truth. Disoriented, I needed to believe something; I needed honesty and truth.

Then, it came. I could not make it stop once I heard each detailed response. My body felt each blow of the impact, and I had only my shirts on the hangers above my head to grab and wipe my tears. It wasn't a pretty sight. The closet was big enough for us both to sit in, but I wanted him as far away as possible, a mere two feet away. I wanted safety, and he wasn't safe. I wanted answers, but I didn't like them. It was time for the truth to come out, and he was willing to share it.

It all made sense in a way. The night's events before the retreat came flooding into my mind. He later shared that the guilt and shame had been building up. As he went to the mountains that weekend, he felt God's Presence, and he knew it was time to come clean. He had planned to talk with someone after and determine his plan for telling me. He couldn't live a double life. He felt tremendous shame that he couldn't stop these behaviors with his own willpower, and he certainly didn't want to hurt me. He feared telling me would cause me to leave. I still don't know how or when the truth would have come out if the Holy Spirit had not done His work that night.

I was absolutely crushed as he shared with me that he was having two affairs. The women had both shown interest in him and made him feel important—a feeling he deeply desired, and a hole he was looking to fill. Confirming my worst fear and validating my intuition, both were women he worked with. My soul was devastated, and with each revealing word, I crumbled a little more. He tried to convincingly share that he didn't want to be with them but really wanted to be with me. He had gone down a slippery slope, and he had "slid" into being unfaithful sexually in our marriage. But even during our divorce, I wouldn't ever have believed he was capable of such a betrayal. He also claimed they weren't emotional affairs, though I had a hard time believing that. He did admit to me that he knew he needed help, and he didn't want to lose me or our family again. He was ready to make some calls and do whatever it took.

That night was tremendously long. Much confusion gave way to shock and disbelief, then deep sadness. All I could manage to do that night was to get a few hours of sleep. The next day was the last day of school for 9-year-old Connor. He had an end-of-the-year performance, and I stood in the back of the room in a daze. My mind was almost numb, but my eyes followed his movements. I wanted him to see I was there for him. I wasn't going to have this taken from me or from him, so I even mustered up the courage to talk to a few people.

Kevin spent that day talking to our pastor, our church counselor, and another close friend from our home group. He was ashamed to share what he had done, but in a surreal way, he felt freedom. I learned later that this scenario is common for couples experiencing betrayal: One spouse's world comes crashing down under the burden of betrayal, while the betrayer, after bearing the weight of much secrecy, has that burden lifted off his or her shoulders.

I remember thinking that I didn't want this burden. It wasn't mine in the first place. *I never asked for it, and you can have it back.* Though this was my human response, and I was alright with feeling what I needed to feel, I knew that God's response was likely different. Matthew 5:8 says, *"God blesses those whose hearts are pure, for they will see God."* Kevin's loving Savior was celebrating in heaven that he had come clean, exposing the destruction not only to his marriage but also in his relationship with the One who could bring restoration and peace to all those broken places. I was willing to let that thought in: God was celebrating the return of this prodigal son and his embrace of the truth. Kevin was able to be there for me a little bit, and he was incredibly remorseful. It felt right to not punish him and add to the shame he already felt.

The evening following that first disclosure, he decided to share more information that was critical for me to know and had been withheld the night before. There had been two additional affairs. One was while he was in school. I had wondered about his study groups at the time, but I wasn't one to snoop, keep questioning him, or worry about something I wasn't sure of. I had asked about it on a few occasions, but I had taken him at his word when he said we were doing well and that there was no concern with classmates. He had the other affair while I was at home with the three kids, trying my best to adjust and settle into our new life in Arizona. Though we had struggled at that time, as well, I had genuinely trusted his fidelity.

Looking back, it all feels so cruel. I had always wanted to take people at their word, and that included Kevin. Hearing about this tsunami of deception made me feel pretty stupid and naïve for a few days. I felt like I should have caught on much sooner. But then I came to the realization that the truth had simply been actively withheld from me. This was not a failure on my part.

The following weeks, however, were grueling. Some days, I could barely get up, shower, and eat. During our divorce, I had lost a lot of weight on the "divorce diet." What was I to share now, when my pants all needed belts, my face looked drawn, and my eyes were swollen? The allergies excuse couldn't explain away all that, and I could imagine the startled looks I'd get, if I said, "Oh, this is the 'infidelity diet.'" But I desperately wanted to protect my kids, then nine, four, and two years old, from knowing about this, at least for the first few months. I was doing what I could to be a somewhat present mom and try to meet their needs, and it was beyond challenging. It was unfair that one of my greatest joys—parenting my babies—I now had to do *again* with great suffering in my heart.

Kevin was in the process of finding help. He began attending a Twelve-Step group, he went to a counselor regularly, and we were looking into options for possible in-patient care. Neither Kevin nor I knew much at that time about this world of support, but I was extremely grateful that he was finally ready to get help.

That said, our reality was that for four of the five and a half years since we'd remarried, Kevin had engaged in on-and-off-again relationships with other women. I've come to realize I'll never completely know the answer to how this could happen and how he could have lived in secret that long. How could he leave the house each morning and come home to sleep each night as if nothing had happened? He didn't even know. While it is baffling, I now know that I don't *need* all the answers to why and how.

We didn't know what the future held, but we kept an openness about the situation nearly every day. We chose an in-house separation, and I asked Kevin to move into my son's bedroom. We didn't want our children to have to carry this big burden on their little hearts, so Kevin would go to bed there late at night and wake up early in the morning. It might sound secretive, but I have no doubt that handling it that way worked best for our family. Some people might say that we needed to share openly with the kids, but they were small, and with the remarriage, I was adamant that we should try to protect them from it for the time being.

It still breaks my heart to think about the turmoil they probably already felt in our home. I couldn't fathom giving them more to process. Connor had already gone through one divorce. I imagined spreading wings around him, and I sometimes tried to pick up that God-sized burden, but I most often laid it back down again. God is a much better provider for my kids, but some days, I wondered how I would survive this. The worry would take me literally to my knees in prayer. I'd lock my bedroom door and cry out to God, tears running down my face. Though my faith was strong in Him, I wavered in fear from time to time. Knowing God would protect the kids was the peace that truly brought me comfort.

Protecting my heart from further emotional damage inside

my marriage and unhelpful reactions from outside my small circle of friends was imperative. At first I told only two people about the infidelity. I added a couple more in the succeeding months—primarily friends who had been through similar situations. I chose not to tell my family or closest friends, believing that their deep desire to protect me would result in anger.

Honestly, I couldn't handle any additional feelings. Mine were enough, and they were colossal at times. Processing other's thoughts, feelings, perspectives, and opinions would have been too much. Though many people loved me dearly, and would have done anything for me, what I needed during this crisis was to focus on my kids and my marriage, keep life as uncomplicated as possible, emotionally, and find clarity within myself, with God as my anchor.

CHAPTER 8

Battle To Surrender

I began to see a new therapist weekly to help me process through the trauma. Those sessions brought me the strength, validation, and comfort that I needed. The one-on-one support helped me make sense of what was in front of me. But months after the initial discovery I still didn't know what my plans were regarding my commitment to the marriage.

This time, I had a clear "Biblical out": Hadn't Jesus himself named sexual immorality an exception to the call to marital faithfulness? (Matthew 5:32; 19:9). But I remember, on many occasions in prayer, asking God what He wanted me to do, and I never felt released. I didn't sense He was asking me to move ahead with divorce or leave the marriage at that point. Sometimes this baffled me, and other times, it made me downright ticked. It was a confusing state to be in.

I desperately wanted to know God's plan, but I also wanted to escape the depths of my pain, something I felt would be easier to achieve through a divorce. I have spent many hours studying Scripture to better understand God's direction for marriage and divorce, not just the direction from those that had given their perspective over divorce.

I found myself digging into Malachi 2:14;16, *"You cry out, why has the Lord abandoned us? I'll tell you why! Because the Lord witnessed the vows you and your wife made to each other on your wedding day when you were young. But you have been disloyal to her, though she remained your faithful companion, the wife of your marriage vows. For I hate divorce! says the Lord, the God of Israel. It is as cruel as putting on a victim's bloodstained coat, says the Lord Almighty. So guard yourself, always remain loyal to your wife."*

Though I had earlier believed that infidelity was the only cause for divorce acceptable to God, this verse (and other verses) gave me a deeper perspective and understanding of the cruelty that a spouse can bring to another and what I believe can also be grieved when divorce is necessary.

Just weeks after discovery, I read a devotional by Oswald Chambers, titled *What's Next to Do?* The title certainly intrigued me, and I clung to these words on the page:

"If you yourself do not cut the lines that tie you to the dock, God will have to use a storm to sever them and to send you out to sea. Put everything in your life afloat upon God, going out to sea on the great swelling tide of His purpose, and your eyes will be opened. If you believe in Jesus, you are not to spend all your time in the calm waters just inside the harbor, full of joy, but always tied to the dock. You have to get out past the harbor into the great depths of God and begin to know things for yourself—begin to have spiritual discernment." [1]

This devotional was followed by a scripture: *"If you know these things, blessed are you if you do them," John 13:17.* Who wants to cut those ropes of comfort and familiarity? It was certainly not in my nature to go "out to sea on the great swelling tide" until I could hear "of His purpose." Nevertheless, that devotional presented me with yet another moment of choice: I had only known God personally for eight years, and I suspected that there was so much more of Him to know. I grew to rely on Him more than I ever had in my life, but I didn't yet know the depths of God.

I did know He had a spiritual journey for me, and if I paid attention and chose to follow His lead, He was going to show me things He wanted me to see. Seeing the depth of Our Savior blows me away and sometimes rocks me to my core. Not only did He show me the way and what He wanted me to see, but He also showed me Himself, the actual gift of Him. I pray I never put the depths of God in a box and be satisfied with a shallow faith. How I would miss out!

My husband continued to rebuild my trust by going to recovery meetings and finding sobriety from what we later coined as a form of love addiction and love avoidance leading to compulsive sexual behavior. We often wondered if this form of compulsive sexual behavior was a qualifier for sexual addiction support because he did not struggle with pornography; though pornography use can bring the same depths of destruction and deception to a relationship. Both are devastating. We came to realize that sexual addiction had different dimensions and aspects and addiction support was just as vital for Kevin. Such support was especially important because he still worked with two of the women with whom he'd had affairs.

This was one of the hardest parts of this whole nightmare. Kevin had ended both relationships with these women the day after disclosure. One was recorded on the phone and later shared with our counselor for accountability. The other took place with me on the line, silently listening. It was the most surreal phone call I've ever been on. I was ready to rage at the thought of what she knew about me and our family and still chose to do. To be totally honest, I wanted to yell some pretty deep and cruel names at her as I sat silently shaking on that call. Of course, I wasn't completely naive, especially now. He could call her back an hour later and start it all up again. For the moment, though, I felt a little morsel of trust being rebuilt, giving a small amount of confidence that he wasn't just giving me words.

We considered moving, even out of state, to find him another job. Kevin gave me that option, but thankfully, our wise counselor at the time told us, "Your problems go with you." He was so right: Wherever Kevin had gone, thus far, there he had been. (One of my favorite slogans now is, "Wherever you go, there you are.")

Moving, then, was not the answer. But he was still going into battle every day at work, wondering if he would see the women, and you can probably imagine what raced through my mind each and every day, when he came home. It was a bizarre mix of relief that he was facing the battle and a low rumbling of anxiety permeating my body—a constant reminder. I couldn't get through more than 20 minutes of my day without getting hit with it again. It was painful and draining at every level.

To combat that anxiety when he was at work, I asked him to call me if either of the women walked by him or talked to him, which he did. But it was really hard to talk about that and be on the other end of the phone line, knowing there was nothing I could do. I couldn't make *them* leave their jobs, and he couldn't quit his job because I was home with the kids. So, these requests were a safety measure for me, and I began to ask for what I needed without apology. Thankfully, Kevin was willing to honor my requests to help me heal.

CHAPTER 9

Truth Revealed, Trust Rebuilt

In June 2009, two weeks after some of the dust had settled from the initial crisis, I was trying to make sense of everything I had discovered. Unsure I would ever get the whole story on these affairs—when they occurred, what led to them, and why—I did what most betrayed partners do: I asked questions. Lots of them. I'm certain now that doing this without professional support for each of us wasn't the best approach. But hindsight is 20/20. I was doing the best I knew how.

I asked Kevin for full disclosure, in part to enable me to clearly process what had happened, and in part to encourage him toward full honesty, transparency, and truth. I knew this would not enable me to fully understand the motives behind his behavior, but it would give me the greatest safety I knew how to get and help me avoid going back to him later with more questions when something came up. Though each answer cut me, emotionally, like shards of broken glass, I know today that a disclosure that trickled in would likely have caused me more harm, so I am grateful for what discernment I had in those disorienting weeks.

During the disclosure process, I sat with my computer on my lap and asked questions, typing in his answers. The part of me that loves efficiency asked for dates, names, and details. There was no shortage of inquiry. Even his thoughts at various times were included on my list. I felt like I needed all the information I could get to begin healing. I didn't want to allow any room for doubtful thoughts to creep in.

Even though it was hard for both of us, my DIY disclosure gave me time to process his infidelity with a clear mind. I began to get a sense of why he acted out in certain ways. I saw how the slope had become slippery until he slid to points of no return. I felt a small sense of empathy for him, and at some moments, I was able to separate the behavior from him as a person.

I realize that men are not always willing to share in this way, so Kevin's willingness to do so clued me into his commitment to do what it took to save our relationship. Though the details of his behavior hurt me terribly, he had never wanted to hurt me, and I could see that.

An odd sense of closeness came as he revealed who he was. I began to grasp that his behaviors weren't about me; they weren't even about sex. They came from the deep wounds he carried. In moments when my anger, disgust, and shock stood still, it was really sad to glimpse his reality. His ability to share those parts of himself gave me some sense of comfort, and I was able to start forgiving.

Forgiveness is, and always has been, a process for me, not a one-and-done deal. I've heard many ways others define forgiveness. For example: "letting go of what has been done to you and giving that person grace," and "moving on and forgetting about it." I believe the principle of letting go is important, but it never quite resonated with me to just let go and move on. There was a piece missing for me. I've learned to greatly appreciate forgiveness through another lens offering three dimensions. I have adapted the concepts of what I learned to help them relate to betrayal and deception:

> *Release Another.* This is letting go and trusting that a process can take place between the person who has done wrong and God. It is allowing that person the opportunity to reconcile the wrong with the God of the Universe, Who has offered ultimate forgiveness through His grace. It is believing that forgiveness can be requested and received beyond us, beyond our awareness, and beyond our human relationships.

> *Release Me.* This is freedom for me and you. This is the choice within our own hearts to forgive another person for the hurt or harm they have caused without excusing the person's behavior. We can choose to move through a process of forgiveness in our own time, which often includes grieving what we have lost, including dreams and hopes that were shattered. We can gain an understanding of and compassion for the wounds and hurts that drove the offender to the damaging behavior. Yet forgiveness does not mean all the pain has gone away; it is, instead, a choice to move through that pain while releasing the resentment.

Restore Us. This process involves both the offender and the offended. The person who has caused the hurt steps forward and attempts to restore what was broken by making an amend. An amend is much more than offering an apology and moving on. It must include not only sorrow for the pain that has been caused but also *reparation*: The offender must turn from the hurtful behavior and put the offended person above oneself, with the intention not to continue the hurtful behavior.[1]

The last element of the process—restoration—is not often talked about. It is a two-way process that often must happen before one can move forward with the other person. It allows both the wounded and the wounding person an opportunity to turn the pain into growth and step toward a stronger and healthier relationship. While conflict and hurt are a part of life, they can, when handled appropriately, also help both parties develop a deep level of empathy. The choice to pursue restoration makes lasting healing in relationships possible.[2]

I have often been a restoration-minded person. I have always sought reconciliation in broken relationships—but sometimes I've done so to my own detriment. I've taken full ownership of wrongs and confusing situations for the sake of moving on, because I despised the discord of relationships that weren't buttoned up and amended. I now have learned to recognize and receive the gift of determining what is mine and what is another's in order to create clear, direct communication and boundaries, which are helpful for many of my relationships. Seeking the first two phases of forgiveness—releasing another, and releasing me—can provide tremendous freedom, and free me to wait if necessary for the final relational piece. God, I have found, has plans even in the unresolved, and my boundaries keep me healthy and whole in the waiting.

It is said that "one of the saddest effects of relational betrayal is the foundation of mistrust laid into our belief system."[3] Trust has been the trickiest part of marriage for me. I tend to give it freely in most relationships, especially when I recognize that there is great potential for giving and receiving love. However, once that foundation cracks, fractures, or crumbles, it takes much to build it back up. Trust requires something of us and is only felt as much as it is given.

Giving is imperative when it comes to broken fidelity in marriage. While I had a choice that was mine to make—to stay or leave the relationship—I gave myself time to make that decision. I observed his behaviors and was determined to give Kevin an opportunity to build trust once again. Either way, I was also determined to give myself the best chance to heal, and to secure my future, moving forward.

As I considered the effects of the broken fidelity, the Holy Spirit gave me a vision of a bridge that had been built and then fallen. Even the strong pillars that had held the bridge in place had completely crumbled. Some pieces had fallen straight to the ground, but others had plummeted into the water below. This represented the effects of the devastation I had experienced and pointed to the reality that it would take time to rebuild a strong and secure bridge. I also realized this bridge couldn't be built with our hands alone. It depended on God, first, and then on Kevin's alignment with God's plans. God was so present, I began to believe that the bridge had to be built again, and that my responsibility was to seek God rather than depend on Kevin alone to rebuild my trust. Soon, the bridge rebuilding task looked achievable, but also proved to be very challenging.

A period of rebuilding followed. Kevin attended recovery meetings and maintained sobriety for an extended period. Our bridge continued to take shape. It seemed miraculous that on most days, the fear, doubt, and painful memories that I had once typed into my computer had faded. God was replacing them with growing confidence that Kevin would never act out in that way again. It was refreshing. It all seemed behind us.

And that's when things really got shaky again.

CHAPTER 10

God Turns The Tables

*"You can enter God's Kingdom only through the narrow gate.
The highway to hell is broad, and its gate is wide for the many
who choose the easy way. But the gateway to life is small, and
the road is narrow, and only a few ever find it,"
Matthew 7:13-14.*

Three years in, in early 2012, Kevin's Friday night recovery
meetings were "getting old." He felt guilty being gone each week,
and I had made it clear that I wanted him to figure out his crap
and let me know when he was "done." I had attended my own
recovery meeting once or twice early on, but then decided it was
more important for me to keep things running smoothly at
home, maintain our family's privacy, and protect the kids from
the burden they didn't need to bear.

This decision led to a slowdown in my own healing and a
lack of staying on track of my vows not just for my marriage but
my vows to myself. I continued speaking with my counselor
occasionally as well as those few who knew of our situation and
I now had relationships in my life with my small circle of honest
and vulnerable friends from church who truly kept me

accountable and grounded even when I felt justified to wander in my thoughts.

Before I share this next situation and potential stumble of my own, I want to share that, at this point in my journey, I had decided to be committed to the forward progress of our marriage and to see the benefits of us staying together. I had given myself permission the past few years to think about my choices, including the option of ending the marriage and whether or not the effects of the infidelity were forever irreparable. At this point, my answer and vow to myself was *I will commit to this marriage the best I can and do all I can to heal myself while holding the standard of extreme fidelity for Kevin.*

Yet, pridefully thinking *I could never do what Kevin did*— fixate on another person outside our marriage— began within a few months, starting with a benign thought of *I wonder if he is a good husband?* Contemplating thoughts of what life could be like married to a particular male volunteer on my team jolted my soul and gave me a sense of escape on hard days. The thoughts were fleeting to begin with but increased in frequency to a few times a day. They weren't sexual in nature, so I began to rationalize there wasn't danger. One day, I was sitting in my backyard with my trio girls—three of us who met to read, pray and keep each other on track—when I knew in my spirit it was time to share this with them. I had withheld it for weeks. I felt embarrassed and a desire to justify myself. I knew it wasn't ok. I knew it could get dangerous if my thoughts became fixations on someone else and they were headed in that direction. These friends loved me well enough to seek more understanding and eventually tell me boldly that he and I needed to be on different volunteer teams. I knew that was the best decision and I felt a deep sigh of relief. My heart felt humbled by this experience that could have been a grave mistake.

Time passed and for months following, I consciously declined my thoughts if they creeped in.

———

At home something, once again, had begun to feel off in our marriage, as though the wheels were coming off the tracks again. With all my heart, I believed Kevin was now faithful in our marriage, so I couldn't understand what else could be wrong.

Then, after an argument with Kevin while trying to figure out what was wrong, I found myself searching for answers in yet another time of uncertainty. Was he back to compulsive behavior or seeking love and attention outside our marriage? Why was he responding the way he was? It all seemed too familiar, and despite feeling a deep longing for answers from God, no answers came. The determination to trust Him was in my mind, yet I mumbled under my breath so many times: *Why God? Why more? Why again?*

I searched online that evening for groups to help with sex addiction and love addiction—my search focused on *him* and what help I could find for *his* issues. It was then that an ad for a book I had heard about from a few people popped up on the computer screen in front of me. I had experienced God's firm kindness and care for my heart for some time, but in this particular moment, the Holy Spirit's conviction hit me right in the gut.

The next day, I went to a Barnes & Noble bookstore and searched in the Christian Religion and Self-Help sections to find a well-known book on codependency. After searching for some time, with my head low, I asked the young kid at the counter if he could help me. I was terrified he would judge me, though, in retrospect, he likely didn't care what book I was looking for. He led me straight to the Recovery section. In my embarrassment and shame, I pretended I knew where it was as I shooed him away as quickly as possible.

Smack in the middle of the shelf, right below the *Recovery* section sign, was a stack of about six copies of the book, facing outward, staring me in the face. I grabbed one quickly, paid for it, and headed straight out of the store.

I often wanted to throw that book against the wall in frustration, yet I couldn't stop reading it; it was a hard read. But it helped me by sharing other people's stories and how they learned from their reactions in destructive situations. They weren't crazy. I came to see through its words that, due to all the marital distress, I had become emotionally hyper-sensitive. I was bursting into anger when hurt. I was focused on his issues, and I'd lost the resiliency I had built early on. I didn't even trust myself anymore.

Let me offer a caveat, however, by saying that although the book helped me recognize some of my behaviors that resembled codependency characteristics, I was also experiencing trauma and attachment distress in the most primary relationship I had as an adult. I do not agree with the contention that codependency within me in any way caused Kevin's addictive behaviors. In truth, his propensity for addictive behavior was established long before we met and would ultimately have contributed to marital infidelity on his part, no matter who he married.

In August 2012, during another argument with Kevin, my deeply held beliefs pushed me to a critical point. Fearful and desperate to understand why our marriage did not seem to be moving forward, I hurled these words at my husband: "You have cancer, and I'm just sick. Figure it out!" I truly believed these words but wanted to take them back the moment they came out. Maybe it was the look on my husband's face or the shock that those words had actually been spoken. I had believed them for so long, probably all along. I somehow knew at that moment my thinking was skewed. It felt awful to say those things, let alone believe them.

Early the next morning, sitting at a picnic bench and repeating those words to a close friend, I could see I was comparing—his wrongs versus my own. With a shocked look on her face and not leaving much room for a pause, she fired back: "So, you think he has cancer, and you don't? Hmmm. Maybe he has lung cancer, and you have melanoma?" I knew then that I still wanted Kevin to take on the responsibility for the sickness in the marriage, or "cancer," as I had identified it. I also knew something had to change, and it was time I flipped the mirror around.

One of my favorite devotionals in those days shares the danger of comparison.[1] As we compare, we place ourselves and others on a ladder—some people one rung up and others down a rung or two. This mindset leads to superiority/inferiority thinking no matter how you look at the ladder. I now imagine sitting in a circle with others chairs across from and next to one another. This permits everyone to be exactly where they are without judgment or comparison. There is no room for us to keep things level or fair, which had previously been a way of life for me. Fairness had been ingrained in my core from an early age, yet I began the process of disassembling my ladder through humility and a bit of embarrassment.

Back in the summer of 2009, after discovery and disclosure, I had attended two Twelve-Step meetings. At the time, I didn't think it was for me. But in the week following that conversation with my friend at the picnic bench—with considerable trepidation—I began Twelve-Step recovery.

Although Twelve-Step recovery might not be the right choice for everyone, I believe it was the best way for me, at that time, to find support and encouragement, develop humility, and experience spiritual awakening—a combination I likely would not have found elsewhere. While it has been the experience of some, I am thankful to say that I was not harmfully labeled. In fact, I bucked the word "codependent" on many occasions. The deep relationship with the Lord and understanding of His abiding love for me that I enjoy today could have been missed had I not gone to those meetings. "Recovery" and "Twelve-Step" work are sometimes considered taboo and stigmatized in our society, but contrary to the stigmas, there I found one of the most hard-hitting, yet beautiful healing processes in my life thus far.

I realized that Kevin and I had been on the scenic route in our marriage and in our lives together. We hoped to see God's beauty and guidance along the way, and that we did. It wasn't always as we hoped it would be, but He had continually asked me to leave that to Him and not worry about where we were supposed to be. *"And we know that God causes everything to work together for the good of those who love God and are called according to His purpose for them,"* Romans 8:28. Though this Scripture does not say what happens to us is good (as far as pleasure), it does promise that all will contribute to our good and benefit us as we love Him and His purposes. God will use every experience to make us more like our Lord—*if* we surrender. And it was high time for me to do just that. And as I chose to lay down my ideals, face up to my shortcomings, and become willing to see life from a deeper and richer perspective, God did for me what I could not have done for myself.[2]

PART II

Persistence in Waiting

"Yet I am confident that I will see the Lord's goodness while I am here in the land of the living. Wait patiently for the Lord. Be brave and courageous. Yes, wait patiently for the Lord."
Psalm 27:13–14

CHAPTER 11

_____

Stepping Forward

A few short months after attending my first official Twelve-Step meeting, I actually began working the steps of the program. I found a sponsor who was willing to commit to this journey with me and to see the underbelly of my character defects and shortcomings. Once I commit to something, I want to see it through, and that perseverance helped me cement this decision. Though there were times when I wanted to throw in the towel, I chose to press forward one moment at a time, determined to see what else was possible in my healing.

The first step of Twelve-Step recovery asks us to "admit we are powerless over our addictions and compulsive behaviors, that our lives have become unmanageable."[1] Life had definitely become unmanageable for me, and I knew I didn't have the power to change it. I was, however, ready to do my part by accepting that I was powerless over others, especially my husband, our past, the marriage problems, my pain, and even my own reactions. Nothing changes if nothing changes, and I hadn't changed much in recent years, at least regarding my personal recovery efforts in the marriage. Regardless of what my husband was or wasn't doing, my life wasn't working for me. I had finally begun to take my focus off of him and free myself to refocus my attention on the one thing I could change—me.

My denial of my own powerlessness had only prolonged the pain. I was now ready to turn over every stone to recover. My anger hadn't helped me get my way, or deal with my hurt. It had only masked underlying feelings—fear, grief, regret, shame, embarrassment, and jealousy, to name a few—that I didn't want to feel or face. My emotions could become unmanageable in an instant, especially when my husband was dishonest. This largely unmanageable part of my life had started to infect other areas, and I was weary.

I didn't find an easy or instant cure. At first, I just wanted to get to it, and get it done. "How quickly could we really get through these steps?" I asked my sponsor. She replied with a smirk on her face, "I'm glad you asked so that we can go slowly now." That backfired, but I needed that wit and humor as I faced the wild terrain ahead.

Albeit with some resistance, I chose to take the time I needed to make progress, little by little. I couldn't complete the steps overnight. Nor could I change overnight. I reminded myself it would take time to uproot my long-held patterns and behaviors. That truth brought me much hope. My hope had previously been in external change (people, places, and things). But this new way of thinking turned all that upside down. Now, change was coming for me!

At this time in my journey, I often found myself in the land of "what ifs" when considering "what then" was so much more helpful. I spent my energy focusing on thoughts like, *What if*

Kevin relapses and goes back to old behavior? How will I survive that? I learned to reframe my thoughts: *If Kevin relapses and goes back to old behaviors, what then can I do to help myself overcome and heal from that pain?* I came to rely on the Lord to fill me with His grace during trials, even if I couldn't understand why I was experiencing them. I shifted from trying to change others to allowing our loving Father to fill me with love for them, no matter who or where they were.

I learned that the process of surrender involved the 3A's: *awareness*, *acceptance*, and *action*. I spent a lot of time slowly finding awareness by God's grace[2] but then I would want to move quickly and directly to action. I remember many moments of trying to apply acceptance to my connection with Kevin. Working as a nurse, he served others all day, putting their needs at the forefront of his mind and intentions. During this time, I worked part-time, but I was at home with the kids almost full-time. When he came home, he would say "hello" and give us all a hug or a kiss, but then, he often moved on to the list of things he needed to get done at home. From his perspective, there were things to be done *for me* and that was sufficient connection for him. I, on the other hand, had a need for adult conversation after the long day with the kids, and wanted his attention. I was his wife! I was keenly aware that I had *asked* for this repeatedly. And he'd *said* he desired to meet my needs, but often, it would not happen. I deepened my acceptance that, if my needs were task-oriented, clear, and understandable, he would respond with more ease. But when my needs related to emotional ties, his brain would glitch, reinforce his view of me as a sort-of enemy, begin to shut down and sometimes get him snappy or mean.

Instead of jumping directly into action, trying to justify why this was important to me, and getting upset, *again*, until he realized it mattered to me—or simply staying busy myself—I realized the importance of acceptance: accepting that there was a pattern, and Kevin wasn't prioritizing change. This allowed me to take care of myself and choose other actions that would better serve me. Acceptance peacefully opens the doors of action.

Another area of personal growth was choosing gratitude over negativity by focusing more on what had changed instead of simply reacting to hardship. Thankfulness began to cover my trials, hurts, and hardships, slowly shifting my perspective on reality, where fear, pride, and self-sufficiency had blinded me.

When I tried to make a decision in Step 3 to "turn my life and will over to the care of God"[3], I felt apprehension. *Was God big enough to take this?* I wondered. The God I knew was big, but my situation had seemed bigger.

God is clear about trusting Him in His Word, in this reminder from the Apostle Paul: *"Each time He said, 'My grace is all you need. My power works best in weakness.' So now I am glad to boast about my weaknesses so that the power of Christ can work through me,"* 2 Corinthians 12:9.

At this point, hope, sanity, trust, and recovery seemed possible for me. However, there seemed to be something unique about our situation. Few in my recovery group could relate to my particular situation—relationship and love addiction with infidelity—so this was still hard to discuss with them. For me, it always felt so personal, and unless anyone I tried to share it with had been in the same or similar shoes, they either gave advice or stood there not knowing what to say.

Sometime in May of 2013, however, I heard about another recovery program that specifically related to those affected by another's compulsive sexual behavior.[4] I had gone back and forth in my head several times about joining that group, while looking at its website. My husband also hadn't been to a meeting there, yet that group was specific to compulsive sexual behavior. In fact, I hadn't heard him say he was an "addict" before, but then again, he had not shared a lot of his recovery with me. Would I be labeling my husband if I attended the group? Was I even eligible for this group? I almost fell, again, into the trap of trying to see if I belonged based on my husband.

When I walked through that meeting's doors for the first time, my heart beat in my throat. I wondered if others could see my quivering hands. But after asking several questions, I realized I belonged. It wasn't my job to label or not label my husband. I had been affected by his compulsive sexual behavior, and there was healing to be found with those who had experienced similar betrayal. I was not alone!

I'd never liked being in the spotlight or drawing too much attention to myself. But staying in the background as the victim in my marriage was a role I didn't want to choose anymore. I could now talk about my story instead of my husband's story. A part of my life had been affected by my husband's choices and struggles, but that wasn't my whole story. I had plenty of other areas of life to open up further and look at character issues. Maybe these imperfections were glaring to others, but I was finally willing to see them myself.

Making a "searching and fearless moral inventory" of myself, however—Step 4 of the Twelve-Steps—intimidated me.[5] My higher power, Jesus Christ, quickly reminded me that this could be gentle, and nothing would leave me in a worse place than before. The process was about taking the time I needed to let the Holy Spirit determine what needed to stay and what needed to go, similar to cleaning out an old house. Don't get me wrong. There were days—sometimes weeks—when I wanted to skip ahead of a few things, but I remembered the word *searching*, to thoroughly look for something more. I imagined that taking an inventory was something like writing a book: you know it's going to take a long time, and you know you're touching on a lot of situations, characters, environments, etc., but you can only write it in chunks. I tried this approach, and between those chunks of doing my step work, I treated myself kindly and gently.

When it was time to read my inventory to my sponsor (Step 5), I was more anxious than I had ever been with her before, but I left feeling so much liberty and lightness. Speaking the truth about these experiences to another human being broke me out of the chains I once lived in. In Steps 6 through 8, I "became ready to have God remove all these defects of character," humbly asked Him to remove them, then "listed all the people I had harmed" and "became willing to make amends to them all."[6] Then I faced Step 9, actually making those amends—that is, admitting how I had wronged others, and acknowledging the harm that I had caused, without mentioning any wrongs they might have committed, and then doing what I could to make things right.[7]

I can now personally say and believe the words from what

has come to be known as the Ninth Step Promises: "If we are painstaking about this phase of our development, we will be amazed before we are halfway through. We are going to know a new freedom and a new happiness. We will intuitively know how to handle situations that used to baffle us."[8] I had clung to those promises, and now I was seeing them come true in my life.

I discovered that the problematic areas of my life that I often knew were there actually had names and definitions. I was able to claim them instead of labeling myself, so they could no longer claim me. As a result, those character defects lost the power they once had in my life. Many of my shortcomings don't show up as often anymore, and others I still humbly ask God to remove. During my time working on Step 9, a devotional passage really spoke to me:

> We hand over to God every moment of disgrace, every tear we have ever cried, every word we wish we could take back, all the broken promises, the loneliness, all the dreams that died, the broken relationships, our successes, and failures—all of our yesterdays and the scars they have left in our life ... When we give God the past, He can make up for all we have lost. He can rid us of the shame and fill the empty places in our hearts.[9]

Despite dreading making amends for the consequences of my character defects, I found this aspect of the work just another step. There was certainly vulnerability and caution when I had those conversations, but gripping fear was conspicuously absent. Much to my surprise, I made my first amends to my husband, even though a few years prior, I wouldn't have thought I had much to apologize for. Each amends was specific to each relationship, and I chose not to share the entirety of my story with each and every person, including the parts about my marriage. I wasn't ready to tell more than one or two people back then. I just focused on taking responsibility wherever possible.

Many have walked this path before me, and God provided a way. "For our earthly fathers disciplined us for a few years, doing the best they knew how. But God's discipline is always right and good for us because it means we will share in his holiness. No discipline is enjoyable while it is happening—it is painful! But afterward, there will be a quiet harvest of right living for those who are trained in this way,"
Hebrews 12:10-11.

I never thought I would be grateful for the difficulties in my life, but I am. They gave me the chance to find out that restoration really is possible, one step at a time.

CHAPTER 12

Healing the Wounds

About seven years after the discovery and disclosure, Kevin and I had found a tremendous amount of redemption in our lives, both individually, and in our commitment to our marriage. We had rebuilt many of the broken pieces and rededicated ourselves to staying together "until death do us part." There was no longer any desire, on his part or mine, for divorce, even when things were not where we wanted them to be. But we still had a ways to go in the area of connection and healthy attachment.

Many of the abusive tendencies and the neglect, on Kevin's part, were being overcome, and I saw that. The sharpness and snappy tones of voice were less frequent. There were compliments about my appearance when we went on dates. The critiques of my cooking, laundry-folding, and even weed-pulling stopped. (Who knew there was a "right" way to pull weeds?) We spent a lot of time praying, seeking, striving, and grappling while also having times of rest and celebrating how we had progressed. If you hadn't guessed already, we felt like battle-weary warriors. But we could often talk calmly now—that was progress—and be in prayer over each other.

That said, we still wondered why things weren't where we

knew they could be. Kevin said to me one day, "I am not ready to settle with where we are." We both knew how to fight for things we wanted and had learned how to passionately pursue God. Surely, He would show us. The resulting fight/pursuit wasn't always pretty, but it was worth the battle.

That passionate pursuit, for me, focused on that powerful, three-pound organ called the brain, the center of activity for thought and understanding. It connects thoughts, feelings, and sensations through our nervous system to our entire body, and, therefore, it can be significantly affected by trauma. Traumatic memories and triggers are seeds stored deeply within our brains that hold information for later use to keep us safe. These memories and triggers are held in the file cabinet of our brain called the hippocampus. When that file cabinet gets too full, however, those memories can be so numerous and vivid that they no longer help ensure our safety but rather, leave us feeling that all of life is unsafe.

I had heard of EMDR (Eye Movement Desensitization and Reprocessing)[1], a form of therapy done by trained professionals, which takes the effects of traumatic memories and lightens the stress associated with them. I must admit, EMDR really didn't make sense to me at the time. It sounded a little quacky and abstract, and my logic couldn't quite wrap itself around the idea. I had always believed I had power over my mind, but when those involuntary responses occurred, I began to think differently. I learned what a "trigger" was and how the present moment wasn't just about that moment but about something from the past getting activated, making the present moment feel much bigger. When Kevin would commit to calling me while traveling out of town for work and that phone call didn't come as scheduled, I would experience a sinking sensation, like the floor fell from below me and my stomach was closer to my throat. This was the same sensation I had repeatedly felt when Kevin had broken his word in the past. I remember a few times when he was at a work conference and had one of those fancy dinners after. I knew those dinners could run late with many people at one table. They would get talking and Kevin would lose track of time. But that rationale didn't matter to my traumatized brain. He called later than expected, and when he called I was swallowing the lump in my throat, trying my best not to cry or scream at him, listening to his "Hello, how's your night?" while also putting on my pristine detective skills to discern over the phone whether he'd had alcohol—not a particular problem in our past—whether he was with anyone of concern, and whether he even realized what this had done to me.

Needless to say, these triggers brought me courage to be more open-minded about looking into this therapy modality and I had heard from others that it had worked for them. The connections of neural pathways in my brain had been wired through trauma, and they needed some rewiring, and I found it fascinating to have tangible science and therapeutic methods to help unbind the stories I had told myself.

There is also a tremendous amount of research out there, regarding the effects of trauma on the body. In the long-term, marital strife, infidelity, addiction, and lack of emotional connection can leave lasting scars. I was intrigued to learn more about the complexities of the effects of trauma through my own healing journey; however, that knowledge didn't come until I had hit rock bottom, physically. I had gone ahead with those two major surgeries to remove the risk of breast and ovarian cancer when my body wasn't in the best shape because there was trauma recovery work that still needed to be done. Hormone changes followed the second surgery. Doctors told me I would feel menopause immediately; however, that was not the case for me. I guessed that the remaining baby fat from my daughter was storing pockets of estrogen to hold me over for a while, sparing me any hot flashes, night sweats, or the typical array of other symptoms. Given that, I thought I was just fine. I have heard it said before that "fine" is an acronym for "feelings inside, never expressed." That was certainly true from my body's perspective.

Though I wasn't completely oblivious to my physical health, it certainly wasn't at the forefront of my mind, nor was it my top priority. I had received much spiritual healing followed by emotional healing in my life over the past several years, and my physical healing process began to show the impact of not being cared for. I had grown up playing sports most of my life and played volleyball at the collegiate level until I was injured during my freshman year. My body gave out from the wear and tear of years in club sports at highly competitive levels of play. I was used to putting stress on my body and letting it tell me when it was finally done. *Done* is the keyword, meaning not when it started to fail but when it had no more to give. That was to my detriment.

Worse, I not only have high pain tolerance, but I also didn't have the best sense of when I was starting to feel bad. I wanted to push through, like I had been taught to do in sports, but some of my drive could also be attributed to a youthful sense of invincibility. At 18, I had major back surgery with the attempt to fuse my vertebrae together due to stress fractures. The doctor's predictions were leaning toward a successful surgery but that was not the case. The vertebrae did not fuse as planned and that was the end of my playing career. Oh, to have truly listened to my body, starting at 18 years of age!

Fast forward to when I discovered the affairs in my marriage almost 20 years later, at the age of 37. During that time, two years after my hysterectomy, my body started to fail from the hormone loss. At that point, my levels fell so fast that I almost flat-lined on all hormone-level tests. I didn't know what good felt like on most days and did only what was necessary, physically, to get by, from day to day. I often had hot flashes and headaches, and my stomach was in an uproar. I felt symptoms that I hadn't felt before, but I just pushed through, thinking it was due to the marital crisis and all the stress. I chose to focus on emotional healing, a semblance of mental stability, and connecting with God spiritually.

Knowing nothing about my personal life at home, one doctor put me on an antidepressant for the hot flashes. I am not opposed to anti-depressants for necessary purposes, but I didn't feel comfortable with what he prescribed, right from the start. I took it anyway, because I wanted to feel better, but then decided to take myself off them abruptly, after spells of dizziness and nausea, which was undoubtedly not the wisest choice. For the first time in my life, I felt like I could claw someone's eyes out while I was simply driving down the road. Antidepressants are serious medications and need to be taken with caution. My resentful thoughts about Kevin combined with withdrawal from the medication, thankfully, came to nothing.

———————

But the months went by, and I began to feel worse and worse. Chronic headaches, which I managed with Tylenol, were a daily occurrence. That caused rebound headaches, and the cycle was vicious. By mid-2010, I decided to visit a naturopath doctor to see what sort of help I could find. My health struggles felt exhausting and not even worth my prayers some days. *If Jesus could heal others so quickly, why wouldn't He heal me? Why was there more for me to suffer?* I didn't have all the answers from God but I was ready to accept I was not as okay as I had led myself to believe. The naturopath helped me find relief from the hormonal symptoms I was experiencing, even making some progress toward relief from the headaches.

I was finally caring for and prioritizing my body more than I ever had before. While my physical health still, sometimes, got pushed to the back burner, I became more diligent about taking care of myself—mind, body, soul, and spirit. All those years of neglect, however, were catching up with me.

———————

Because of my hysterectomy, I believed I did not need to get a female exam and thus, 7 years passed until a visit to the OB-GYN I won't forget. A seemingly routine visit resulted in finding out that I had contracted HPV (human papillomavirus)—the most common sexually transmitted disease in the United States, impacting millions each year—sometime in my adult life. I was wrecked and did not know where to turn. I did not know about the high statistics, nor did I know about the possibility of cause, dormancy rates, and treatments. I felt so much shame, yet another scar of wounds from my history. The truth is that I will never know where this came from. *Could it have been my two previous sexual partners? Could it be from Kevin from before we met? What about during our marriage? What about the affairs?*

The reality was that I was very cautious to use protection prior to marriage, as was Kevin. However, during his affairs, he took risks. The virus could have sat dormant for years (or even decades). I had no way of knowing. After that appointment, Kevin got a frantic phone call, a myriad of inquisitions, and hysterical emotions as I needed answers once again. I needed confirmation that there were no new behaviors that caused this, which he provided safely to me. I needed his care and his compassion. I needed to better understand if he had more information. He sat with me and took ownership of his recklessness. He felt the sting with me. My body was taking the brunt of what may have likely been his doing. Each year we grieve this reality and celebrate when it does not show an active virus. I do my best to be consistent with my exams and keep my immune system as healthy as I can as that is a factor in it staying dormant.

As for my gut health, it had been a mess during the years of seeking deeper connection in my marriage and remained troubling even after some years of trust-building from Kevin. With the constant counseling, grueling discussions, and regular arguments, my body was now appealing for the change it deserved. It was crucial that I look at myself as a whole person instead of trying to assess symptoms individually. My bones had lost density tremendously from the lack of hormones, and my thyroid had been attacking itself, an autoimmune condition called Hashimoto's Disease, since 2005. My Hashimoto's flared in 2010 during the headaches, and in 2015, I was diagnosed with a form of irritable bowel syndrome called small intestinal bacterial overgrowth (SIBO). Autoimmune conditions are highly associated with betrayal trauma in women, and I was no exception.

I was crushed at the thought of tackling yet another area of my life. At the young age of 43, I not only had a marriage that was still shaky, but also a body that was a hot mess as a result of what it had been through. I was grateful that it wasn't life-threatening serious, but I still cried outside my doctor's office on many occasions as I was coming to terms with the fact that God wanted me to care for my body. I wasn't too happy with God for bringing something else my way, and I was speaking harshly with Him. I know He heard me just the same, and I was okay with being mad at Him, as long as I could move through it. Besides, it was too soon to give up. I had a lot of life to live and really did want to be healthy. So, despite how I felt about it, I committed to it, knowing God would carry me through as he had so many times before.

Under the effects of the autoimmune condition and the SIBO, I felt pretty cruddy most days. Fatigue, irritated bowels, and headaches were the result for months. There were some big changes I had to make with my diet to get rid of the bacteria. I saw a nutritionist, and she put together a food plan for me for 30 days. Honestly, it felt like starvation some days with how strict it was, and I lost a good bit of weight even though that wasn't my primary purpose.

Given the strict dietary regime and the resulting need to prepare my meals, I often prayed while cooking. It was a tough season because Kevin and I were still not at a stable point. Cooking had already been a tender topic for years. His unsolicited-advice would play in my head: "You can do it this way to have it taste better." So, I pressed within to find moments of encouragement for myself. Thankfully, after some tough weeks, the majority of my symptoms subsided, and I am grateful to share that I am still on track toward health today.

Six months after completing my first journey through the Twelve-Steps, God and a potential sponsee prompted me to begin the steps again around my own sexuality. With familiar justification, comparing, and doubt, I pushed back, internally, against the prospect of beginning again, especially in an area where I felt more like a 13-year-old: immature, unaware, and scared. There was a need within me to minimize, and try to rationalize my way out of, starting again, because I couldn't visualize the outcome—there was no way for me to know whether things would be the same or different. My fears aside, I also knew that it was high time I looked into, and then conquered, my issues around sexuality. The prospect of becoming a sponsor, and helping others, also drove me to address this area of my life using the steps.

CHAPTER 13

Seeking Authentic Sexuality

My own sexual issues had pre-dated the infidelity in our marriage. It was long before that and even before meeting Kevin. I hadn't wanted to look at it deeply for years, but I've since learned that once I decide to do the hardest stuff by choice, I see the greatest reward. In the end, I yet again accepted my powerlessness and unmanageability and got to work.

My initial journey through the steps was very thorough, seemingly slow, and took some deep, deep thought. Now, I didn't hurt people or control them quite like I used to. I cared about others but didn't live in their pain or their insanity quite like I had before. I cared for myself much better. I knew how the process worked, and I trusted it. So, this time, the process was a little gentler than the first.

Amends also came more naturally. I didn't have to struggle to disguise or deny my weaknesses anymore. I knew that when I messed up, I could start over and not be ashamed. I could let others make mistakes, too, without finding fault in them either. In fact, we do a lot of "re-dos" in our house now, and I hope it will always be part of the culture in our home.

This round, I was asked to journal my sexual experiences.

That has probably been the single most terrifying homework assignment I have been asked to do in my life. For the sake of vulnerability (a core value of mine), I did what I was asked, and it taught me a lot about who I was. I had a false core belief that I was not normal—different in some way. There was fear of standing out or being embarrassed. It had been an area I had hidden for years both from Kevin and from myself. I truly didn't know my desires or even what it was that made me feel set apart. I had been living in status quo, sexually, and I knew that God had more for me and for us.

We had discussed likes and dislikes a few times, shared our preferences, and had some adventure mixed in. But I had often felt he had sexual needs in our marriage that were far greater than mine, and I just obliged him and tried to enjoy it. Really, I just couldn't seem to figure out my own needs and desires apart from his. I could relate to the following quote from a book that debunks societal messages about sex, especially the notion that it is our job as women to please our husbands first. "But for many women, sex initially moves at too fast a pace and steps are skipped. Their bodies never had a chance to say, "I need this!"[1] Truth is, I never gave myself a chance to go backward or even slow down to put myself first.

Before marriage, I knew well the two people I had sexual relations with, I cared for them, and, I felt, they cared about me. My perspective was that sex was nice but didn't need to be as pleasurable for me. I played it safe, so as not to risk too much in these relationships. Playing safe, however, confused matters once I was married. My premarital relationships were shallow, with no real level of intimacy or true love. Though I had consented on all occasions, sex never amounted to much in the way of connection. There wasn't much thought about the long-term effects of early sexual experiences, aside from the precautions taken to avoid pregnancy. I know, now, that fitting in was more important to me than doing what was right or better yet, caring for myself.

As for my marriage, from the earliest times, I remember feeling desired. I never felt objectified sexually and was never pushed into anything uncomfortable. The problem was what I *was* comfortable with. I never wanted to withhold sex because I believed that was a need for Kevin. Based on The 5 Love Languages, Kevin had love languages of physical touch, acts of service, and words of affirmation. But my love language was mainly quality time—emphasis on quality.[2]

Our pattern became something like this: Eight out of ten times, I would realize it had been a week since we had been together sexually, so I would attempt closeness. Given my need for quality time, I would often ask for it, schedule it, and lead it. Then, I would feel temporary closeness, and we might talk or connect for a minute or two after, but then he would fall asleep quickly or move on to something else. It would feel abrupt, transactional at times, and I wouldn't know what to do or say. I'd feel uncertain and sometimes confused, at first, then get used to it. I had often heard a way to a man's heart was what happened *after* being sexual, but that baffled me because that was not the case for us. Though I had these feelings and shared them early on, I gave up after repeating myself for so long. But those experiences still felt empty. There was nothing that seemed to draw us closer in a lasting way.

My confusion escalated over time, and because I had never talked about this with anyone, I experienced some shame once I began this work. It still puzzles me to think about our society and why peer groups, church groups, close friends, and families shy away from any discussion about healthy and empowered sexuality. At forty-two, it was about time I began owning and knowing who I was versus what I felt I was supposed to be. No one else was critiquing me (not even Kevin), and I realized that I could choose not to be the one—and worst—critic.

Over the years, I never overtly blamed my husband for my sexual insecurities, but I did subconsciously hide behind our history as an excuse for not spending time on this area of growth for myself. I really didn't think about it much, but I now know that can be what denial is all about. We did have more pressing issues in our marriage earlier, but now, I had an opportunity to determine who I was fully *and* sexually as I tenderly asked questions of myself.

"Obviously, I'm not trying to be a people pleaser! No, I am trying to please God. If I were still trying to please people, I would not be Christ's servant," Galatians 1:10. I still laugh at the Apostle Paul's use of the term *obviously*. What a sense of humor! The Lord knew all too well that some of us would try to please people over God. I certainly was trying to shift that thinking in my life and please God by working the steps around my sexuality.

I embarked on a journey toward a better understanding of the behaviors I was choosing. In recovery, we use traffic stoplight colors—red, yellow, and green—to describe different kinds of behavior and the effects they have on us. *Red-light* behaviors are those that have caused us pain and that we are responsible for. Sometimes, they are our most destructive behaviors.

My first red-light behavior was to avoid speaking up for my needs and desires sexually, and the second was having sex when I was not emotionally connected. Designating these behaviors as red lights implied I wanted to stop doing the behaviors and, instead, pick up some *green-light* behaviors. Green-light behaviors included not taking myself too seriously, becoming more adventurous and open-minded, engaging in laughter and lightness, identifying my absolute "noes," asking to be held until I know what I want, stopping to pray, and remembering to accept myself exactly where I am. They sound easy on paper, but that middle warning area was what often got me into the red-light behaviors. Once I saw *yellow-light* behaviors arise, I knew I had a choice to pick up a green instead. My yellow-light areas were not knowing how I felt or what I wanted, living in the land of "I don't know," making "I should" statements, having feelings of doubt and immaturity, using passive-aggressive actions instead of asking for what I needed, manufacturing my connection emotionally, and letting my fear of being seen by others as mean, bad or unfair drive my decision-making or leave me indecisive.

Once I was able to look at my past, determine why things had unfolded in the way they had, and get it all out in writing, I began to feel the shame and confusion lift. I shared my experiences with my recovery friends and with Kevin, who had, thankfully, created safety for me to share and to be heard. As a result, I felt a release of shame and realized *nothing was wrong with me*. My sponsor showed genuine compassion, a true gift.

And because I was able to own my behavior and patterns, Kevin was able to hear me differently, to not associate what I was saying with his own faults and past actions, and to avoid jumping in to try to fix things. He had been hearing from me that this was a raw space to share and explore together, and he often shared his appreciation of my willingness to know myself better so that I could share it with him. Freedom for me to get to know myself allowed me to share myself in unity with my husband in a way I never had before.

That said, these broken, learned patterns had been playing out for a very long time. In consequence, we are still searching for, and striving toward, where we want to be sexually and how best to connect with one another. We must continue to communicate about our desires and preferences so as to not fall back into old behaviors. Though it will never be perfect, our sexuality has become a means of truly and authentically connecting.

CHAPTER 14

Maybe When I'm 93

"Recovery is dependent on trust in God and obedience to His Will for our lives."[1]

If you had asked me even eight years ago if this next part of our story would have been in this book, *I would have said absolutely not.* There would have been no way in which I would have wanted to share that about which I carried heaps of shame. A story that was from before we met. A situation that is still surrounded by uncertainty in my mind.

Kevin and I have talked at great length about whether or not to include it. There was concern it might be confusing in the middle of my story to include something that happened for him before I even knew of his existence. Yet, ultimately, I chose to bring this part of our story into view because it illustrates what I now believe are three foundational principles for a healthy marriage and family:

1. *Keep no family secrets.* Secrets separate, overburden, and ultimately isolate those who keep them. I've worked too hard in recovery to even think of keeping a family secret

now.

2. *Don't carry another's shame.* No matter when or how another's secret comes to light, it is harmful to others' souls to assume a share of the blame.

3. *Take no action on delicate topics without discussion.* Leave no one out who might be affected by what is shared. There is nothing like the grief that comes when one is left out of the decision-making process.

Here's the story.

It was a simple question: sometime in 2013, a gentleman at the local gelato shop asked Kevin if he had been in the armed forces. In front of the kids, he answered honestly, "Yes, the Navy." I had been trying to determine what flavor of gelato I wanted, and if I was going to take into account my dairy intolerance, but suddenly, I didn't feel hungry anymore. I stood there in disbelief, with a look of surprise on my face. It was incredibly hard to not have been consulted about something so delicate to me.

Connor was now thirteen, Tyler, eight, and Katelyn, six, and we hadn't shared anything about his time in the Navy with the kids before. *Why?* He had received a dishonorable discharge after spending time in military prison for arson at the age of 20. Sadly, he was then a young adult who had served two years honorably prior to this incident, but desperately wanted to feel seen and important. Toward that end, he lit a small can of string on fire, intending to put the resulting small blaze out and be the hero. The motive was neither malicious intent nor harm. But the fire got beyond his control and caused damage to military property. With little thought to the consequences before and after the incident, he confessed, without legal representation, to starting the fire and served two years' time with an early release.

We had told very few people about his time in the Navy because that part of the story might elicit too many questions. I certainly hadn't shared the story except with a few trusted confidants, and we had concurred, years ago, that we wouldn't discuss the Navy at all with the kids until we agreed upon a suitable time. I had no idea why he had chosen to do so now, without consulting me! Needless to say, it was a sickening drive home for me.

Later that evening, I asked him to talk with me about it. I needed to understand what had happened, to have some explanation. He said something to the effect of, "I didn't think it was a big deal," and then casually informed me that he had shared that he had been in the Navy with the boys a few months earlier while away with them for a weekend in Tucson. *And hadn't even thought to tell me before this moment?* I was shocked and panicky, fluctuating between numb and irate. I hated this subject more than anything else! *Had I carefully avoided talking about it for this long only to be left out of the conversation completely when my own kids were told?*

In hindsight, the kids received this news without flinching. As they heard what Kevin said, they continued to pick out their favorite flavors of gelato. I think it may have even gone over Katelyn's head at her young age. Nothing more was shared with them until many years later with the occasional mention of military appreciation and on Veteran's Day.

Though keeping this secret was mostly about protecting Kevin's image, I now see that there was clearly a benefit for me. That my husband and my children's father had been to prison was something I kept close to my chest because I believed that I would be judged and looked at differently. I wasn't even in his life at the time of the incident, but I, somehow, had picked up some responsibility for it, as if it were *my* problem, *my* story, *my* prison time. "What's wrong with me for choosing a father for my kids who would do this?" I demanded of myself.

Looking back, my unwillingness to talk about it probably brought on more shame for both of us. I feared that the kids would face confusion and uncertainty. If we didn't bring it up, we could avoid that. I felt I could shelter them and protect their hearts. I hadn't considered the possibility that God could protect their hearts, should that news be shared—that finding out this way might actually be part of God's plan for them.

I've since learned that the Lord doesn't want us to live in secret, including keeping those family secrets. I now firmly believe that the Lord brought that gentleman to the gelato shop that day to free us, build our trust in Him, and help me see Who had the better handle on my kids' hearts. Kevin and I experienced a tremendous release from the shame we had carried for more than two decades. Psalm 103:12-13 reads:

"He has removed our rebellious acts as far away from us as the east is from the west. The Lord is like a father to his children, tender and compassionate to those who fear him."

I gained a deeper and abiding trust in the Lord. I chose to lay down my fears at the foot of the cross and walk in obedience, one step at a time. And I think about not just my story here but also about all those for whom religion and belief in a God, presented in an unrealistic, harsh and judgmental context, was, and is still, part of their trauma. Maybe some have even had a person or a well-ingrained belief that added to a spiritual bypassing injury—using spiritual principles or ideals to dismiss those emotionally and psychologically distressing situations. I remember for a long time that I had spiritually bypassed thinking the Scripture "… *don't let the sun go down on your anger* … " Ephesians 4:26, taking it out of context. I simply took it to mean, *Don't go to bed mad, Shawna.* I'm not sure if the idea came from my husband, myself, church culture, or somewhere else, but it dismissed my justified anger and sadness over the whole situation.

God wasn't just saying, *Get over it Shawna*, but He was also saying, *Don't let it get out of hand or stuff it either*. Oh, how I realize it may take time to unwind twisted messages. For that, my heart breaks for those injured by these harmful dismissals. If you find yourself holding your breath reading this, please take the time you need. There is no rush. God continues to wait patiently for me, and He will do the same for you.

<hr>

There were seasons when I would find myself face-down on the floor in my bedroom, so close to the carpet that I could smell the years of dust in the fibers. With tears dripping down my face I wondered why God hadn't seen my pain. *Was He ever going to intervene just for me? Just on my behalf? Just because He saw my wounded-heart?* I wanted to see how it would all unfold and how He would be there for me no matter what *before* I'd be willing to believe something was possible.

There were many areas of my life in which I had come to fully trust God's goodness, but that was not yet the case in my marriage. I related to Thomas, the apostle who refused to believe that a resurrected Jesus had appeared to the other apostles until he could see and feel, firsthand, the wounds received by Jesus on the cross. Like Thomas, I was skeptical, refusing to believe without direct personal experience and proof what Jesus could and would do.

Could I trust God alone? That was the big question I pondered and dissected from lots of different angles. *What did that even look like?* God gave me the depth and creativity to look at things deeply. I've sometimes wondered if my natural skepticism is a character downside, but I choose to believe God built me for pondering. God expects that we will experience doubt, but when we remain in doubt, we aren't completely turning it over to Him. It was hard to reconcile myself to the thought of Him expecting us, in our humanness, to do something *without* full confidence. But trusting Him more required me to lay down my life and the outcome of my marriage. My grip began to loosen. In the Bible, Matthew reminds us,

"Then Jesus said to the disciples, 'If any of you wants to be my follower, you must put aside your selfish ambition, shoulder your cross, and follow me. If you try to keep your life for yourself, you will lose it. But if you give up your life for me, you will find true life," Matthew 16:24-25.

My marriage was that area of life that the Lord wanted me to see this whole process in a bigger picture—to have a glimpse of His sweet plans for me and find true life no matter the result. I found some deep clarity: Previously, I had been willing to stay in the marriage for the time being but not at all costs. I had been waiting for the miracle of growing closer to Him and didn't want to leave before it came. Kevin was addressing the destruction and devastation, and ultimately, I believed God wanted more for us. I was waiting for someone who would have empathy for me, cry with me, grieve with me, feel with me. I desired someone to love me deeply. But maybe that person wasn't Kevin. It was God. Kevin and I were two people willing to commit to the marriage, but God wanted me to trust Him alone, and I wanted to learn how to trust Him fully before I took any other action. Trust is "assured reliance on the character, ability, strength or truth of someone or something; one in which confidence is placed; dependence on something future or contingent."[2]

During a quiet morning of reflection, after that day at the gelato shop, I chose to lay myself down for the sake of my marriage and became willing to walk through the waters, even if they became murky. I knew that if we both laid it all before God, we would be okay. I'm grateful the Holy Spirit led me to that desire, ultimately, to put my trust in God alone, because I didn't have a searchlight into the future. And that trust would be soon tested.

Sadly, less than a month later, Kevin misled me greatly once again. He was working an overnight shift at the hospital, which he didn't often do, and I was concerned for his safety driving home the next morning. I slept well that night trusting that he would get a few hours of sleep before driving home. I was no longer concerned about him being with other women; he had built a lot of safety there, and I believed that he was not acting out. When morning came, he called on his way home from work across town a few hours past the scheduled time for his shift to end. So, I gathered he'd gotten some sleep. But then I asked him a few questions about his sleep to confirm he felt comfortable driving home. At first, he didn't give me any reason to believe he hadn't actually slept, and what he said went along with the story from the night before. But he was fumbling his words a bit. So, I asked more questions. After some prompting, he admitted that, in fact, he hadn't slept at all the night before, but stayed up, working all night. Confronted with his dishonesty, he self-justified and defended himself—a familiar guilty response. It was a quick conversation and when he got home, he gave me a watered-down apology and shared he had no intention to bring up that situation again.

I had relied most on trust in human relationships, and Kevin had broken my trust repeatedly. Since I'd recently made the choice that my trust would be in the Lord, I didn't want to doubt God's goodness at this moment. I also believed a strengthened marriage would come from this. Maybe I would be 93 years old when it did, but it would come. But what about Kevin? How was he to come to the same decision? The answer, I realized, was to be found in my own experience. I had come to trust Him because I had suffered the consequences of distrust. There would have to be consequences for Kevin's dishonest choices. Once again, something had to change.

CHAPTER 15

Defining My Personal Space

Honesty has been a core value for me since childhood. So much so, that I have wondered whether I, a truth teller by habit, could now lie consistently even if I wanted to. I'm not saying, of course, that I'm perfect by any means. When my fear rises up, I have occasionally withheld information to avoid disappointing others. Kevin struggles in a similar way. So, I could now understand a bit more of the "why" behind Kevin's deceit. But that didn't excuse it, nor did it explain the "why" behind his absence of deep remorse and empathy—the part that really hurt. These consistent breeches of integrity brought me feelings of injustice and fury.

I had become familiar with the term *boundaries* in recent years, but I hadn't realized that setting boundaries was the key that would enable me to define my personal space, free me to speak my preferences to others. In fact, setting boundaries was what enabled me to push back on things that I wasn't comfortable with as I was growing up. I think that, to some extent, boundaries came naturally to me in *certain circumstances*, but in others, they were foreign. I also began to learn that boundaries are not brick and mortar walls but fences with gates that can be open or latched shut. Further, they not only function as the limits we set to protect ourselves, but they also define the lines we cannot cross without harming others.

I had set boundaries for myself around Kevin's sexual acting out. I no longer checked his phone constantly or called him to check on his whereabouts day in and day out. In fact, I no longer had the desire to engage in those behaviors (that were once very important for me to seek safety) because he seemed so ready to stop the affairs once he was found out. When it came to the dishonesty, however, I didn't believe he really wanted to stop yet. Duplicity seemed to be ingrained in his character. His fear of getting into trouble had so strong a grip on him that deception had become a long-term coping mechanism. He wanted to be the "good-boy" and not get into trouble, yet he lied.

To deal with that, I had to learn how to set boundaries when wrongs weren't made right. I couldn't just move on and pretend like nothing had happened. I fumbled a little, not knowing how best to both take care of myself and share how I felt about Kevin's dishonesty. I'd emphasize that I wouldn't be the one to tell him how to make amends, but then I'd give him verbal scripts to follow, only to get frustrated with both of us. So, deception remained a recurring event in our relationship.

I knew something needed to change, so I decided to ask Kevin to leave our bedroom as an act of loving myself well by setting and then respecting my personal boundaries. This second in-house separation was an enormous step. It didn't come lightly or right away. It was agonizing. I anticipated Kevin's opposition, but this time, I knew my choice was intended to be a short-term solution. I felt that I could not be in the same bed with someone who would not connect emotionally, be completely honest, see the impact of the choices he had made, and take steps to rebuild trust after further deception. Rather than trying to control him, I was, instead, setting a temporary boundary that would provide me with physical and emotional safety and space.

I also learned to not measure honesty and dishonesty on a scale of best to worst—from truth with a capital "T" to white lies to whoppers. Instead, I chose to stand firmly for what I believed God had called us to in marriage—standards for honesty that were not my own but rather, those from the Word of God. Using God's Word as my barometer for honesty brought the comfort that dispelled my doubts about choosing to separate. I was able to take a firm stand: no lying, no hiding, no omitting information, and no intentionally misleading me. I didn't seek professional counsel on this, and I know it could have gone desperately wrong. My sponsor didn't give me counsel on this decision, but rather pointed me back to God. Maybe that was God's plan, so He would be my Wise Counselor, my complete Comfort.

Kevin was quite riled up when I proposed the separation. As he had before, he felt like I was trying to control him. It was the first time in our marriage, and one of the only times since then, that Kevin did not speak to me for nearly two days. I was familiar with some push back on boundaries, but this was extreme. Our typical pattern—I pursued, he withdrew—had to be abandoned, and this time, I let God handle the pursuit. Separated for 10 days, we both took the time needed to work on ourselves and determine the next step for us as a couple.

During this time of waiting, I took refuge in worship. Worship music became a comforting part of my routine, in my car, kitchen, bedroom, shower, and while doing laundry. It was my escape. It brought me peace when there seemed to be no glimmer of it anywhere else. Knowing each harmony, each rhythm, each chorus, each word was prayerfully considered brought me strength when I was worn and didn't know which way to turn. It pulled me out of deep sorrow and despair when I was on my knees, lifting my head to the One that would truly hold it.

To this day, the work of songwriter Kari Jobe has had a unique and special way of leading me into God's presence. Her song, titled *I Am Not Alone*[1], holds a deep place in my heart. When I looked up the lyrics again, recently, it brought me back to a time I heard it live, with Kevin and the kids only an arm's distance away. That concert was one we almost didn't make it to together, due to a repeat performance of our marital "conflict dance" that nearly kept me home. For the sake of the kids, I pushed through that day. The song's lyrics have become my anthem: I'm okay being alone in my marriage because I am truly *never* alone.

Being alone physically and emotionally in my bedroom for those 10 days was tough. It wasn't what I wanted, but I chose it for the sake of greater things. As had been the theme, restoring trust in our relationship was part of our journey. It was an area that I believed would come naturally *if* I sought the Lord above all else. The thought was that it would come together with time, eventually. But something was still gravely missing, and "something still missing" had been the theme of our marriage for years. Always under the current was a sense of shaky trust we knew all too well. At that point, we kept searching for a closer emotional presence with one another, an intimacy that God had shown me deeply through the storms. We would never have that level of intimacy with another human being, but I knew that God had designed intimacy for the marriage bond. It wasn't time to settle just yet.

It was January of 2014, four-and-a-half-years since our most devastating crisis of trust: the discovery of his unfaithfulness and betrayal. The wounds were nearly healed from the affairs. That work had not been lost on us. Forgiveness, offered, given, and received, was a thing of beauty when we found it. But, like every rare jewel, the cost of forgiveness was very high. Forgiveness as I have previously shared is so often misconstrued—in social circles *and* in the church—that I think it's important to share a quote that stood out to me, from a powerful book that focuses on *Healing the Wounds of Sexual Betrayal*:

> "Forgiveness isn't cheap. When we add up all the hours of pain, worry, loss and devastating financial impact, it's not hard to see how much sexual betrayal has cost us. Most of us know at some point we need to forgive. It's not about if; it's about when. Feeling pressured to forgive too soon creates a risk of burying our pain alive. It's ok to take time to grieve what's been lost before choosing to let it go."[2]

Many couples don't make it through the forgiveness and trust-rebuilding processes after such dreadful offenses, and we were keenly aware of the statistics, especially since our risk level increased with a second marriage.

During the time we were apart, I made an imperative decision not to take on the responsibility of determining the next step for our marriage: our next appointment, our next counselor, our next whatever. I could have dove right into my old role of fixing it and finding the answers, but this time I was surprisingly content to wait. There was also heartache, for sure. But I knew it would be best for me, and for us, to wait on Kevin's timing. Kevin wasn't able to articulate then what he can now. He didn't need the level of relational intimacy with me as I did with him. He often just followed suit with my needs. If I said I needed to have time to talk to hear about his day, he realized he needed to hear about my day, too. If I needed to be heard about a concern, he realized he needed to be heard, too. His own needs took time to realize *after* he could relate them to mine. Stepping out *first* with his needs and desires would take practice.

Kevin took on the charge and stepped into what he thought might help us. He made some calls and looked at two possible directions. One was a couples counseling intensive that focused on intimacy avoidance for those feeling alone in marriage, a very accurate description for our circumstances.

The second option involved a therapist about an hour away, who is trained in Emotionally Focused Therapy (EFT). The message of EFT is simple: "Forget about learning how to argue better, analyzing your early childhood, or making grand romantic gestures … Instead, recognize and admit that you are emotionally attached to and dependent on your partner in much the same way that a child is on a parent for nurturing, soothing, and protection … EFT focuses on creating and strengthening this emotional bond by identifying and transforming the key moments that foster an adult loving relationship: being open, attuned and responsive to each other."[3]

We could relate to both of these modalities for therapy and support. Ultimately, after much discussion, I gave Kevin the option to choose what he felt God was leading him to. He chose the EFT therapy because it was local, and we could easily drive there for appointments. We had extended therapy sessions weekly for about nine months, along with a short weekend retreat that focused on the more intense areas we couldn't get to in our weekly sessions. It was a very structured process and really resonated with our conflict spiral. We named our conflict pattern the *rugby spiral*, because we met at a rugby match, originally, and the roughness of that sport lent itself to the vicious cycle in which we often found ourselves.

CHAPTER 16

Stuck in the Spiral

Our rugby spiral usually began when I would approach Kevin with an issue or concern I had. If it related to other people or situations, he had a much easier time being present and staying regulated during the conversation. But when the issue I had related directly to him—even something simple, like my desire to feel heard when I spoke, or feel cared for when I had thoughts and feelings to share—the descent into the spiral would begin: He would become sensitive to perceived criticism and dysregulate, often getting snappy and rude as a means to protect himself. I would then become utterly confused by that extreme response and want to defend myself. All the while, my initial concern was ignored. I perceived he would be kicking and screaming so as to not let me in too close. If he kept me at a distance, he felt his vulnerability or wrongs wouldn't be seen. I would get internally triggered by this response, with which I had become very familiar.

I could never understand how we could spiral down so far, so fast; it literally felt like seconds. "Rugby spiral" feels a little inadequate, given how quickly it would all happen. Maybe we should have named it "the vortex" because it was chaotic and would just suck us in.

Kevin had a well-established strategy for pulling away, either by defending himself or by denying responsibility and then diverting the conversation. I, at this point feeling even more vulnerable for bringing something to the forefront, would begin to try to prove my point, often getting angry to protect myself in some way. Things would continue to ramp up. We would then recite past offenses, making blanket statements, and blaming each other. Although we both desperately needed care and affection, neither of us had anything to give the other, so we both dropped into self-protection mode.

Angry outbursts were often a go-to for me when I was hurt by those closest to me. I didn't get angry with many others in my world, but when I wasn't heard by Kevin, it would hit a raw spot. I believed, in my anger, that I could make myself safe by yelling or trying to control him. This false reality had been deeply rooted in me from a young age, when I didn't feel heard or respected because my feelings didn't align with the feelings of others. My anger storms with Kevin almost felt "outside" of me and triggered memories of similar experiences from my youth. It was as if I was at a table, and all parts of me were there. My anger was off to the side, not knowing what to do or when to take part. As if it were beyond my control, it would rise up as it had learned to do and was certain to make Kevin feel extremely unsafe.

Through the EFT process, we learned how to better listen to each other. How to give and receive feedback. To hear what the other was saying (rather than focusing on what wasn't being said), and taking it at face value, asking more curious questions, and trying to speak a bit more concisely. We learned how to recognize and then be more sensitive to each other's raw spots—

those more tender spaces—and what those raw spots represented.

This growth didn't develop without a lot of scripting and prompting. This was the scripting that I welcomed unlike the long time resentment I had with Hallmark. Kevin tried for years to script what he would say to me, as if he was copying a Hallmark card verbatim. I later learned he was trying to find the words that did not come natural for him, but it made me cringe each time I would get those scripted cards. I didn't realize how important the individualized words meant to me.

As we practiced our connecting time at home we even imagined having a picture of our therapist next to us when we were having conversations, and we created a place in our bedroom with two "safe chairs," where we would have these hard conversations.

The process was rewarding, most days, and took us to another level, enabling us to communicate in a much more vulnerable and healthy way. We saw that there was hope—that things were getting better in this mysterious area of our relationship. But we also realized that there was no "standard protocol" for finding intimacy in marriage, at least not that we had found. We took this to heart, and gave our all to putting EFT into practice, even after we graduated from our weekly sessions. When we were on our own more, without our therapist, it still held strong for a period of time.

But...life got busy, though I guess it had often been busy with our family of five. But Kevin was working full time *and* trying to obtain multiple college degrees (an act of achievement for him).

Did I mention that he used busyness to avoid connection—sometimes consciously—and that his plan increased after each degree while obtaining *five* post-secondary degrees in college?

In late 2014 and much of 2015, we didn't seem to be in crisis mode anymore, which was a welcome reprieve. Kevin decided, during this time, to work his recovery steps in the area of dishonesty and unleash the grip deception had maintained on his life from a young age. He learned to uproot even mild dishonesty and transform his character into one of authenticity. He was trying to focus on being truthful even when his body and brain were focused on avoiding exposure. I was his spouse, after all, not his parent. I could see the change, and I acknowledged it, knowing that it had taken a lot of hard work to learn a completely new way of relating to others and turning his healthy relational circuits on.

It may have been the Twelve-Step work that he was focusing on now, or that we were falling back into old patterns, as we all often do, but as the months wore on, our emotionally focused therapy work seemed to be slipping. The structure, routine, and moments together in the therapy office had ended. The rugby spiral was ramping more often, and as time went on, we tried to hold on to the work we remembered. For Kevin, it was out-of-sight/out-of-mind, the fade of short-term memory. For me it was an increasing awareness, a focus on what was slipping away. We would take out the workbooks we invested in at the retreat. But more often than not, I was the diligent one, reminding him that we needed to do that work. This re-created some resentment for me, and an "I am a failure" mentality for him. I didn't want to fall back into our old roles—me, the pursuer and him, the withdrawer—so I began to sit back and observe.

Taking on the role of the observer proved challenging. I couldn't be the one pushing all the time, and yet I deeply craved what we had built. That desire never went away, no matter how much I bargained with it. I knew what was possible, and we had done it with the help of our therapist. I wasn't sure why it hadn't stuck, but it wasn't my job, alone, to figure it out.

A passage from the biblical book of Habakkuk was helpful during this time:

"I will climb up to my watchtower and wait to see what the Lord will say to me and how he will answer my complaint. Then the Lord said to me, 'Write my answer in large, clear letters on a tablet, so that a runner can read it and tell everyone else. But these things I plan won't happen right away. Slowly, steadily, surely, the time approaches when the vision will be fulfilled. If it seems slow, wait patiently, for it will surely take place. It will not be delayed,'" Habakkuk 2:1–3.

These verses and the posture of Habakkuk reminded me that if we wait patiently and confidently, the Lord is faithful to reply. A devotional reflecting on Habakkuk's priorities reminded me that "Habakkuk realized that he was appointed as one of the guardians of the kingdom, and he took his place at the guard post. There, he waited and listened for how the Lord would address the wickedness and decay around him. Habakkuk cared about righteousness, and he longed for revival. But he never demanded an answer from God; instead, he appealed to Him for one."[1] Like Habakkuk, I could lament and draw attention to the injustices I saw, but address my lament to God, not Kevin. I could have a humble, but eager heart, as Habakkuk did, and boldly address my "asks" to God, never doubting he would reply. I realized that I could position myself in such a way as to not miss what God might say by sitting at the watchtower of my own circumstances, listening closely, and never demanding an answer from God. Rather, I appealed to Him and waited expectantly, taking comfort in His promises. But it was a delicate balance to maintain!

Though there was discomfort in the uncertainty, I felt encouraged, strengthened, and loved. I knew I was adored by God, and I had others to encourage me. I read God's Word and contemplated it, letting it sink in and transform me. One particular day, God led me to Mark 10:17–31, where Jesus asked the rich man to give up all he had and follow Him. Jesus wanted Christ to be the sole desire of the man's heart and his sole Provider. *What would it mean to give up everything in my marriage?* I wondered. I wrote the following in my journal on December 1, 2014:

> *Give up my power to change things, my circumstances. Give up my needs to God. My need to be connected. My need to feel like a priority. Give up my expectations of Kevin. Expecting him to be accurate in communication. Expecting him to show humility when wrong. Expecting him to identify the defects in his life and amend them. And instead, I decided what I could do. I can submit to God that which controls my husband, his work, fear of failure, fear of inadequacy, dishonesty, sexual/relational integrity, and intimacy*

avoidance. Rejecting the thoughts and feelings that I am alone. Releasing Kevin from obligation to meet my needs. Give up more than I receive. Matthew 10:39 rang true again: "He who loses his life for my sake will find it."

I know that we have an enemy. And that enemy will find ways to take our minds to places that distract us from God's truth and His care for us—putting our marriage relationships above our relationships with Him. I know that, with each struggle in our marriage, the enemy will attempt to deny us success. It has actually become humorous now seeing the enemy's tactics from afar and how very limited he is in his craftiness. He isn't the creator of anything new. In fact, he is a thief: "The thief's purpose is to steal and kill and destroy," Jesus declared in John 10:10. *"My purpose is to give life in all its fullness."*

I believe the destruction of marriages is a top priority for the enemy. And, at least in our case, our marriage was an easy target. Therefore, that day I boldly chose to put the lies of the enemy away from me: that I needed to be right, that I had to self-protect, that we would never communicate well, and that I was superior to Kevin. There were dead, dry places in our marriage that still needed prayer, and I chose to begin praying for the resurrection of those places, for help to shed the armor we had put up to guard ourselves, to put on the armor of God's righteousness that was not our own, to rise out of the details of conflict to the repair, to grow into deep conversation with vulnerability, and to patiently persevere by taking small steps forward. I began consistently praying for my husband and for what became a newfound submission.

CHAPTER 17

The Three-legged Stool

If you had asked me before this relationship started if I could have survived what occurred in the past two-and-a-half decades, I would have answered, *No way! No way could I have been strong enough. No way could I withstand that story. No way could you get me to stay. No way, no way, no way!* So much had needed to happen to prepare me for believing different, knowing different, doing different, and being different. Through it all, I had considered, doubted, reasoned, and concluded that I believed deep within that God had much more for us—and even for me—despite these "no way" circumstances.

These many years had held so much pain, but there were some beautiful moments, too. I didn't want to lose sight of the good: We had spent time on family vacations and taken weekends away as a couple, along with just those simple moments, sitting around a table or on a couch, watching a movie or playing a game of Yahtzee. Traveling through airports, lounging on sandy beaches, and even taking a road trip in an RV through the desert with no air conditioning (that was tough) were all worth it. We never wanted to give up on those moments and good memories. These good times were so special to us because they were moments that might have come naturally for other couples, but they existed in our experience because of our hard work and God's mercy.

One memory that illustrates this paradox is our family vacation to Hawaii in the summer of 2015, the same year I was diagnosed with SIBO. Before we left on this trip, I felt minimal closeness with Kevin. He appeared to be pulling away by staying busy. There was no time available for the deep communication and prayer together that he had recently committed to work toward. I shared the importance of feeling connected before this big trip. The last time we had taken this particular vacation, we were only a few short weeks out of the discovery and disclosure of his infidelity. I wanted our Hawaiian holiday to look very different this time around. He did, too, he said.

The night before we left, he chose to ask me if I wanted to connect at 10:30 p.m., after he had busied himself all day with less-than-relevant tasks that had eaten up the prime time we might have been together. This evening, I gently said it wasn't a good time to start a conversation because it really seemed to me that, at that late hour, we'd just be checking off a box on a to-do list. Well, 48 hours later, we were well into our trip, and he was withdrawn. The more I leaned in, the more he pulled away. I felt it, but I didn't want to grapple with it out of my desperation to seek attention and time with someone who would feel no closer to me than a stranger. When these times came over me, his withdrawal seemed so unloving to me that I actually began pulling away some, too, to guard my heart. I just didn't want to hurt more.

At the same time, however, I knew this wasn't who he wanted to be. I knew this wasn't his heart. I knew this was more of a dry-addict characteristic—sober yet still so self-absorbed. Desiring to protect himself from any closeness.

This was not the timing I had hoped for, but it was, sadly, something with which I was all too familiar: We had saved up to take everyone back to the same location where we had remarried. The resort where we had stayed was stunning and held a special place in our hearts. Coves had been carved out and led to the deep ocean at the end of rock jetties. Just a short walk away was the spot on the edge of a cliff where we had remarried and read our renewed vows.

We tried to hang on to the sweet memories of our first trip, but sadly, we didn't get along. Instead, we "went along" for the kids. We wasted countless hours, discussing our issues and trying to hang on to our marriage, when we could have been taking in the beauty of God's creation. There was one particular moment that I remember being completely paralyzed, unable to see God's beauty. I couldn't reconcile it in my heart and mind. The backdrop of the wide Pacific Ocean was so vast and endless, and yet I couldn't see its beauty. I just couldn't see it.

On the third morning of the trip, as I walked with beautiful palm trees in view, I reached out and made a phone call to a friend in recovery. My heart was breaking from the neglect and the resulting emotional and spiritual starvation. I came near the spot of our remarriage. It was incredibly difficult for me to shift my focus away from the self-absorbed husband, and yet still love the husband I'd remarried and trust my heart to the loving responsibility of God. I knew God would give me the abundance of love and compassion I needed for my heart and Kevin's. I realized I couldn't do any more, given where Kevin was at. But I knew God was asking me not to lose sight of His abiding creation nor the knowledge of what true love looks like. I knew at that moment God was pulling me out of despair and into His deep presence once again.

Right when I think I can't take it anymore, and it's time to give up, there is a refreshing sense that he's got me. "It's not over," He says. "Just get back to focusing on yourself and I will take care of the rest. My Spirit is alive and will do what it needs. Trust me.'"

It became so clear to me that the disease, the addiction, the attachment disorder or whatever you want to call it was so separate from my husband. I truly didn't know what to call it anymore. I knew it was a distance, a deprivation, a starvation, a cry for secure attachment. When I sensed all of that behavior coming to the forefront, I had an opportunity to remember there was nothing to defend. It didn't have to be scary like a stranger coming at me that was unfamiliar. The battle within him was as real as I was feeling it. *It* was trying to come after him, too.

"Staying on your side of the street" is a concept in Twelve-Step recovery that is well known and I bucked it from day one of attending meetings. My side of the street is where I work on important individual issues apart from my spouse, without distraction, allowing healing by the power of God through my diligent efforts. In any relationship, there is also the other side of the street: the other person's work and efforts, done apart from me. But there is the middle of the road that few in recovery circles seem to talk about. I understand it as the space in which the focus is on the relationship. We needed to do much work in the middle of the road, but this tricky work just hadn't come naturally for us. Concerned for and distracted by the complexities of meeting in the middle, I would be thrown into confusion.

I found it helpful, therefore, to change the metaphor to that of a three-legged stool. There is my work toward healing, his, and ours. If one leg is weak, the marriage is unstable. If one is missing, the marriage falls. This put the emphasis, then, where it belonged: on ensuring that all three legs are strong.

My personal work continued to be a spiritual awakening. There were so many layers, and the focus felt eclectic at times. By this time in our journey, I had completed my second round of step work. I wrote this reflection:

> *Once again as I have worked the Twelve-Steps, and my ability to see more clearly what is right in front of me has been evident. I often say God is bringing to light what I need to see, maybe just not always what I want to see. I love what God has done in my life and brought it to my attention. My awakening has been progressive and not at all what I thought it would be. It is so much deeper and stiller than my first fiery crash into the steps in complete desperation and survival. My sexual and spiritual awakening have taught me there are many ways to achieve the same freedom. Different is necessary, and vulnerability is imperative. My Lord, my Higher Power, desperately wants to be with me, guiding me through it all.*

Along with my personal growth work during this season, I was intentional about praying more fervently for Kevin, and doing so with greater frequency than before. I rediscovered a book about prayer that had sat neglected on my shelf for years. I had read most of it but had never finished it. I wrestled with the purpose of praying for him again when I had already prayed for him many times and not nearly as much that I had hoped for changed. I doubted my prayers could help when God already knew the outcome.

I knew Kevin had free agency and that my prayers in particular couldn't stop or start any behavior in and of themselves. Yet, I wasn't just praying for an outcome this time. I wasn't even necessarily standing in prayer for Kevin single-mindedly. Of course, my desire was for change and protection of my heart, but that was precarious. Most of me was praying so that I could draw closer to God and walk with a deliberate yield toward God's heart and His desires for my husband.

I got on my knees to pray, speaking the prayers aloud in the living spaces of our home. These moments helped me find purpose and strength through focused intentional prayer. While I didn't and still don't agree with the all-too-familiar and overly spiritualized authority-based submission to husbands, formulaic framework of prayer, promises of outcomes, and various other pretenses, I do value the stance on being deliberate and diligent in prayer. There are many helpful books on prayer now that weren't accessible to me then. That focus on prayer shifted my perspective toward the things of God and toward certain elements that I had the privilege to pray over.

I prayed specifically for God's restoration of sanity in our marriage. I prayed these words over and over again: *"God, I ask You to take away the armor we have put up to protect ourselves. Help us rise out of the depths of despair in conflict to the heart repair, the raw spots, growing deep conversation with vulnerability and patience to persevere in making small steps forward. Give me the heart for Kevin that You have for him. Get me out of the way so he can be the leader. Remind me of all his great qualities."*

I asked God that Kevin's integrity would be set at a high standard of honesty and truthfulness, that his decisions would be made with patience and discernment, and that his focus would align with his heart instead of obligations. I prayed that his relationships would be authentic and genuine, and his legacy as a dad would be worthy of being passed down. This time of dedicated prayer enabled a shift in my focus, giving me a new perspective that increased my faith despite the compounding losses within my marriage.

Amends continued to be a part of what I did to sustain our marriage. In fact, making amends became a new way to live. I needed to know where my wrongs were and how I could make them right. I might not be able to repair damage done or fix the issue at hand, but I can own my part and make amends as a step forward. I also learned to distinguish between the times I truly needed to take responsibility for actions I had done, and the times I wanted to make amends for things that actually *weren't* mine to own for the sake of not feeling uncomfortable or responsible.

Finding the balance—knowing when to say only what I really needed to say—was a process. No matter how many times I went through my steps, there was always some cleaning up to do. I learned to listen to the nudges of the Spirit, sometimes gentle, sometimes bold. Although the process fell short of perfection, it made it easier to make my amends, and if I was honest, open, and willing to look deeper within myself, I found it beautiful.

Many of the amends I made were with the people I lived alongside each and every day, namely God, myself, Kevin, and my kids. As I chose to seek forgiveness with God, I considered what harm I had done to Him. I questioned, "Could God be harmed by me?" I defined *harm* as 'hurt, broken down, or made less valuable." Knowing God's nature hadn't changed, and He loved me right where I was, I realized I had made God less valuable to myself and others. I eventually wrote my first letter to and from my Immanuel (God with us). This is what we shared:

Dear God, don't know that I've ever written you a letter, but more of thoughts and prayers in my journal. Seems more formal with a letter, or maybe just feels different knowing you're going to write back immediately. You have always known what's best for me and sometimes I've doubted that. Doubted your timing or the outcome you wanted. I love our growing relationship and one that continues to be more personal and intimate. I'm glad you know me so well. At times you have spoken to me when I'm sleeping, and at times you have stopped me dead in my tracks. But no matter what, I know you love me. I think you would prefer to be gentle with me, but I can often make that hard. Not listening to your quiet voice, so I give you permission to be loud when you need to, nudge me out of the way too. And as I continue to follow your will for me, I will try my best to let you be the leader and get out of the way. It's a conscious decision at times, but that's ok, I know I'm just a work in progress, and progress I have made with only your guidance and my reliance on you. I love you my

Lord and thank you for loving me. ~ Shawna

Shawna, my sweet daughter, I do love you! I have seen your progress and I have noticed your hard work. I have been there in times you've been aware of my presence and other times you didn't even notice. I built you and understand the ins and outs of you. I understand your struggles and your hard times. You are NEVER alone. I understand that you may not always feel that, but the reality is, I'm right there. Be still and let me show you. Remember, you don't have to rely on your own way, My way is far better, that's a promise to you. You can definitely do some hard work in your personal recovery and growth, but don't forget the healing and change comes from me. It's a tough balance sometimes between the work that needs to be done and the waiting. Continue to look at me and I will help you discern that. Keep your thoughts on what we've already accomplished together. We have more to do. Much love, Your Heavenly Father.

Letters from God became a way to hear Him more clearly and to bring assurance that I am never alone; He is always with me. I continued with this practice and the work I had already been doing. Kevin did, as well. We kept pressing forward toward healing and hope and into a deeper intimacy with God and one another, while some big decisions for our family loomed on the horizon.

As a personal amends to myself and after much searching and prayer, I found a precious necklace that spoke to me the moment I saw it. It was a token to remind me of my persistent love and care for myself. It had a flat pendant, with a heart cut out of the middle. Around the outside of the heart were footprints. It was as if God was saying, "I am right there with you no matter the emptiness or loneliness you feel. No matter what you have done or haven't done. I will always fill you with my peace. Keep seeking me above all else." It reminded me of Psalm. 59:16–17: *"But as for me, I will sing about your power. I will shout with joy each morning because of your unfailing love. For you have been my refuge, a place of safety in the day of distress."* Could this scripture be our promise of true safety, calm for our dysregulated nervous systems, peace for our weary hearts?

All my amends came with various emotions: nervousness, excitement, relief, and trepidation. I had made amends to Kevin before, and I hesitated this time around, because I knew I would still mess up in the future. Why make amends for things I may likely do again? Sure enough, I have on many occasions since that day made mistakes that needed amends, but I am glad I didn't miss out on giving that gift to him and to myself back then. My amends to my kids have turned into some amazing times together as I work to show them I am flawed and make poor choices, too. The silver lining in all of this is a home where accountability is given and received regularly. We don't often like it when we are the one who gets called out, but we wouldn't have it any other way.

As for Kevin and his leg of the stool, he continued to do his recovery work and to seek God above all else. Sometimes, he admits he would pick up the tools of counseling or recovery and forget that what powers the tool is the only One who can bring life. He would lean not on the Giver of the tool, Jesus, but get stuck in the process. There were times when giving up would have been easier—throwing in the towel as he once did before—but he has committed to us and to God. What matters to me most is that we are now both willing to passionately pursue God above all else and trust in the greater purpose. Without that, there would have been no chance of us surviving this crazy ride.

As for the stool's third leg, our support when we're in the middle of the road between our sides of the street, Kevin's broken attachment issues from early years needed some work on the scaffolding of our couple-ship. While we were in a more advanced stage of needing support to be able to naturally flow in our conversations and connection, we still had some groundwork to lay. The couple-ship recovery became the more challenging leg to manage because we were still both working to support our own legs of the stool. Those legs had to stay strong to enable us to do work together. We were each committed to getting to these places that still needed healing. We chose to work on more EFT with a new therapist, our fourth therapist on this journey.

Because we weren't often able to meet together for these new EFT sessions, learning how to navigate with the therapist over the phone was new territory. Our therapist gave us appropriate work to do together to strengthen our emotional and relational commitments. We spent time each day sharing feelings, praises and affirmations of one another and dedicated prayer time.

It was a starting point, designed to create the connection that wasn't a natural response for my husband. It was more of a formula for him to establish a routine for relating. It helped him initiate in a way that made sense to him and it also created something I had longed for: closeness. I could handle a few days of missing our time together here and there, but when these moments were forgotten consistently, I felt heartache. Through it all, I had to be willing to be *available* for emotional intimacy but not *pursue* it, while Kevin worked to come toward me in the best way he knew how. To acquire that willingness, however, I had to undergo one of the toughest transitions in my recovery.

CHAPTER 18

Boundaries and Detachment

The willingness to be available to, but not to over-pursue another in a relationship was something I needed not only in my marriage but in many of my other relationships as well. But it required a form of *detachment*. Detachment is defined by the American Psychological Association as follows:

1. a feeling of emotional freedom resulting from a lack of involvement in a problem or situation or with a person.

2. objectivity: that is, the ability to consider a problem on its merits alone. Also called *intellectual detachment.*[1]

My greatest desire in relationships tended toward the opposite: *secure attachment*. Closeness, connection, agreement, safety—*these* were my definitions for a good relationship, especially with my husband. How could detachment possibly help *me?* Frankly, overt detachment in the form of avoidance was the *less than ideal circumstance*—something my husband was very familiar with, and the cause of one of our most difficult relational struggles.

Detachment and its role as a positive relational tool took me a long time to figure out. Multiple things complicated that process: There were some areas of my life where unhealthy attachments simply weren't an issue. When it came to making decisions about where to eat, who to go to the coffee shop with, and what I wanted to do, I didn't struggle. I did have a voice, and often, I knew what I wanted. I chose to speak up, when asked, and it felt genuine. When it came to more significant decisions like the next best thing to do after hurting feelings with a friend, I struggled to stand secure in my relationship with that person. I waffled between avoiding the conflict for sake of peace or saying something with hopes of restoration but fear of the disapproval of the other person lay at the root of my struggle. People-pleasing and going with the current "normal" population seemed to bring ease for me in many areas of my life.

Normal, however, is a relative term. Normal to one person might not seem normal to another. So, for a long time, it seemed to make life easier to just fit in, fly under the radar, and avoid subjects that might cause relational disruption. But that didn't work so well when, to fit in, I agreed to things I didn't want to say "yes" to or felt obliged to make peace simply for the sake of avoiding conflict. Making peace is not a bad thing but betraying myself and my well-being for the sake of peace caused conflict within.

There was also a cost to avoiding disappointment in others. Having to "figure out" each person and then determine what might or might not disappoint them made me crazy sometimes. It was not only exhausting but it also killed authenticity, something that, in my discovery process, had acquired a high value for me. I no longer wanted to lose myself in those moments.

Detachment, especially for those of us who struggle with unhealthy attachment to others, is established and maintained when one sets boundaries. Boundaries and detachment have become so significant in my life that I believe they deserve a special place in the story of my recovery. Learning new ways of relating to others can bring confusion and turmoil, especially when we are pulling away from unhealthy attachments. Giving myself permission to set boundaries and put some emotional space between myself and another have empowered me in ways I didn't think possible. Saying "yes" when I mean "yes" and "no" when I mean "no," have enabled me to walk in integrity.

I learned that it was not my business to assess what others thought of me; it was simply my job to say what I needed to say in a direct, kind, and honest manner, to keep my motives clean and clear, and to focus on the goal of peace and unity, knowing all the while that peace and unity aren't always possible. People do disagree and disappoint each other. I had to "remember, boundaries aren't going to fix the other person. But they are going to help you stay fixed on what is good, what is acceptable, and what you need to stay healthy and safe."[2]

The more boundary work I did around this, the more straightforward, honest communication became a gift I could give, both to myself and to others. But don't think this came by just snapping my fingers and hoping it would happen. I had to make an agreement with myself—set an *internal* boundary—that applied only to me: *Speak up and say what I need to say within twenty-four hours.* This internal boundary usually had to be put into place when something I knew was going to be hard for me to share, and/or something honest yet potentially painful for someone to hear. Interestingly, I could typically do this with those closest to me, namely my family, but friends, acquaintances, and even those I wasn't close to at all, were the hardest. I had to stay within my 24-hour limit any time I caught myself minimizing a situation, avoiding potential conflict, fearing others' judgments, risking another's disapproval, wanting to blend in rather than stand out or be seen as different, risking that others would see me as mean or inconsiderate, wanting someone else to say something I wanted to hear, or feeling compelled to explain or justify myself instead of simply using my voice. When these crazy thoughts and feelings started whirling around, my wild mind could embark on a bit more torturous path than was necessary to get to the point where I could just say what I needed to say (one big reason why I adopted the twenty-four-hour timeframe). Why stay in agony any longer than that when I typically *already knew* what needed to be done?

During that twenty-four hour period, there were "green light" behaviors I could choose to do (and still choose to do, as needed, today) as I gained the courage to be authentic and true to who I was:

- I reminded myself to be honest, to allow for disagreement with others, and to choose to stay in the moment rather than jump ahead to anticipate the response, all the while praying and admitting my need for God.
- I focusing on courage, and rejecting those old messages-to-self ("You're inconsiderate!", "You're mean!").

- I worked hard at meditating on God's Word and memorizing Scripture such as, *"The Lord himself will fight for you. You won't have to lift a finger in your defense."* *Exodus 14:14.*
- I journaled and wrote down my options.
- I made a phone call and accepted encouragement from someone who knew me well.
- I asked for perspective on the problem from someone else.
- I role-played the situation.

Nearly every single time, it turned out that God got me through it:

"My thoughts are completely different from yours," says the Lord. "And my ways are far beyond anything you could imagine. For just as the heavens are higher than the earth, so are my ways higher than your ways and my thoughts higher than your thoughts," Isaiah 55:8.

God could see the end. He knew how it would turn out, and seeing my authenticity is what He always asked of me. It's how He created me.

Today, I'm not convinced that, in the long run, it ever really felt better either to win the approval of others or avoid their disapproval. It might have felt easier temporarily, but I've realized that conflict is a part of all areas of life, not just some, and must be addressed sooner or later. Sooner is better.

To be my authentic self, I had to be completely honest and who I was called to be, even at the expense of disagreeing with others and, maybe, even upsetting them. I have worked boundaries and reworked boundaries over several years. I determine my need, which helps me determine what boundaries I can put in place. That previous shortcoming of disapproval of others was a long-standing issue for me that took some practice, but I could see the reward once I made those hard decisions and chose to stick to my internal boundaries.

Boundaries with my husband have been especially important and our relationship is where detachment has been most often coupled with my boundary work. As I've shared (and, maybe, over-shared?), intimacy was lacking in an overwhelming way within our marriage. It was a game of chase from me to him. We had learned during our couples work that I needed to set boundaries for myself to stay emotionally sane, mentally stable, and relatively reasonable during the times he pulled away. Of all the work that I have done, alone and collectively, this turned out to be the hardest and had to be the most intentional. It was, quite honestly, exhausting to enforce these boundaries. I was weary, but my deep desire for change made it worth it.

Thankfully, some of the boundaries I implemented worked well, and enabled us to make progress in our relationship. I freely shared them with Kevin, because boundaries are not rules—walls to keep people out or me inside—nor are they a means of judgment or a form of punishment. At least I hope they never come across that way. They are, instead, a means for *me* to know when, where and how far I can go in a relationship, and how best to take care of myself during times of difficulty, when I need safety, sanity, and stability. Simply put, they help me stay engaged but not entangled.

They were, however, tough to write and much tougher to

enforce. I quickly learned there was a battle between two systems in my body. My attachment system craved closeness and intimacy, while my central nervous system craved safety. They would be at war, and it was my job to decipher which system should take the lead in a given circumstance. It took some time and practice to become adept at deciding whether intimacy or safety would take precedence, and then create helpful boundaries efficiently.

I learned to set two kinds of boundaries: *relational* boundaries, which allow me to detach when necessary from another person, often to offer me protection, and *internal* boundaries, those I set for myself alone as a form of personal containment. The following briefly describes them and includes my guidelines for each. Although my husband is the "other" in the descriptions, they can be applied in other relationships as well.

Relational Boundaries: External (protection). Think of a hand facing outward, like a stop sign.
- I will share my feelings and perceptions with Kevin when he overtly or covertly distances himself from me.
- I will stay open to discussion as long as negative behaviors are not minimized or justified. Kevin must either identify them or be willing to look at the situation and come back to me to own up to and express a satisfactory understanding of those behaviors.
- I will remove myself from the situation or the environment if destructive behaviors are not being addressed or if the situation escalates.

- I will not do the work necessary to find answers or reconnect.

Personal Boundaries: Internal (containment). Think of your hand facing inward, like an open palm on your chest.

- If I feel unsafe with Kevin, I will walk away, stating that I need a timeout. I will stand firm and will not be pulled back into an insecure environment.
- If chaos ensues after I ask for my safety, I will take time alone to process where I am.
- Anytime I need to, I will excuse myself to do breathing exercises, or hum and sing to regulate my nervous system.
- I will listen to music, pray, or read when I feel I need to and be all right with it when that requires leaving the other person temporarily.
- As a healthy distraction, I will call someone or seek a change in scenery, e.g., take a drive or go for a walk.
- If I neglect to share something, or find it too difficult to share, I will take responsibility for that omission, then commit to sharing it within a reasonable time limit.

Boundaries and detachment impose limits, yes, but they nevertheless function, constructively and affirmatively, to remove what limits our ability to determine who we are in relationships and to speak up for what we find acceptable in our lives in terms of the ways we are treated and how we relate to others. There are endless opportunities to set effective boundaries, and there are many books out there to guide us, but the most important part, to me, is to be honest about my motives when I set boundaries and step back into detachment. Honestly taking my motives to God, asking Him to assess and search my heart, and then cooperating with Him as He helps me to stay true to who He has called me to be—these are the keys that unlock true intimacy and closeness. Ultimately, it's letting Him be my Protector, above all. When I do that, the benefits of detachment surely follow, as this devotional illustrates:

> "For me, detachment is relatively easy with casual friends, where I'm not very emotionally involved. I've noticed that when I am detached, I can listen to other people being critical or grumpy without being affected. But if members of my family act the same way, I often take on their negative frame of mind. My own behavior shows me that I have a choice about my response to other people's moods and attitudes. What I have learned by comparing these two situations is that detachment involves paying attention to my own mood before I have a chance to take on someone else's. Then I can simply see and hear negativity or anger, without becoming negative or angry. I don't have to have a bad day just because someone I love is struggling. This knowledge allows me to let everyone, including myself, feel whatever they feel without interference."[3]

I also had to accept that others might set boundaries for me, too. Others might need to detach from me. Whether they are seeking protection or working on personal containment, it can be hard for me when I don't see it coming. Learning to detach in loving ways is the key. When I chose to distance myself from others, step away, and take care of myself, I hoped that they would respect those boundaries. So, I try to show respect when someone I'm struggling with relationally does what I would want them to respect if it were coming from me, even if I don't like it at first.

Boundaries are not to be taken lightly, especially when they relate to others. One must remember that the boundaries will be pushed, avoided, and might even be mocked, which is why we usually need to set them in the first place. I find that being gentle while putting them in place is a tremendous gift we can give ourselves. With the right motivation behind them, boundaries can bring beautiful life changes and incredible relationships.

When I think about detaching in a loving way, the best picture that comes to mind is gently walking away while leaving a soft cozy blanket on the other person. That visual picture has gotten me through many situations where I wanted to smother Kevin with a pillow. Most times, that would have been more satisfying. Metaphorically, I have done both.

When I wasn't able to be calm, however, I was in a reactive stance. I threw daggers verbally, and although it makes me nervous to share it even now, I occasionally pushed Kevin or slugged him in the arm. I'm not proud of that, but I'm trying to keep the spirit of authenticity I have been mentioning even though I cringed as I wrote those words.

Detachment helped me buy the time I needed to come up with a calm response rather than react and see the situation more clearly. I could pull away instead of spinning on the reactive merry-go-round. I would make a very conscious effort to walk away and provide feedback: "I'm not available right now if you are going to speak to me like that," or "I am choosing to take care of myself for a while. Please let me know if you'd like to reset later." Then, I needed to follow through, and it was so hard taking those steps to leave Kevin's presence.

But I had learned, by this point, that if I stayed engaged and did not separate, I would fall back into self-reliance and impatience, the very opposite of trusting the boundary and detachment process in the situation. I was still called to respect and care for Kevin, even when he wasn't showing me the love and care I was hoping for. If I remained entangled and reactive, the result was likely to be more hurt and disappointment for both of us.

Though they often left me feeling neglected and desperate, I needed to look at those times in detachment as opportunities to draw closer to God and myself. I could be so dependent on Kevin in those reactive moments that I truly missed being present with God, and therefore, was unable to gain another perspective. Again, practice made this easier to accept over time. Although I felt, in those reactive moments, that I could gain some control over Kevin and force him to engage with me, the reality was that he wasn't able to freely choose to be present. I was truly powerless to change Kevin in those moments.

CHAPTER 19

Gifts of a Four-Year Old

Throughout our marriage, we'd had an interest in adopting a child. In my case, it was a dream that would not let up. I had felt for a long time that God had laid adoption on my heart. This deep desire had been clear to me even during times of turmoil in our marriage, and I remember getting angry that it wasn't a real possibility, given the state of our relationship for so many years. I can clearly recall a conversation I had with a close friend as I paced back and forth in our backyard, arguing against the idea that it might not be possible. I wasn't arguing with God, particularly, but rather, against the idea that it might be an unwise and untimely choice at that time. Ultimately, I had to become willing to submit and lay that choice down, although I did so with great difficulty, and only because I knew it was the obedient step that God was asking me to take. After that, I was not quite as sure that it would ever happen, and I tried, reluctantly, to accept that, as well.

One Saturday afternoon a few years after that pacing episode, I remember standing at the kitchen sink with Kevin.

Things were different. We had completed our Emotionally Focused Therapy a few months prior and were putting it into practice. So, I said to him, "Sometimes, I think we should have had four kids."

In a nonchalant tone, with a neutral affect, he said, "We should adopt." I remember stopping and staring at him as he continued washing dishes. He didn't even look up, so I walked away quite perplexed. Oddly, he hadn't noticed my reaction. The next day, I asked him if he was serious. He replied, "Yes, I think I am."

We certainly had some healthy-sized conversations about it after that. And at that time, we hadn't seen a lot of reprieves in our marital struggle, so the fact that we could simply *discuss* something this significant, without descending into conflict, was welcomed with joy. Adoption felt exciting, scary as heck, and was looking like a real possibility at that point.

As the two CEOs of the family who had "get it done" as our strengths, Kevin and I began the application process with an adoption agency a few weeks later. It was a Christian organization and one that had come highly recommended. We truly felt God was leading us to grow our family in this way. We had lengthy discussions with the kids and, although they expressed a variety of emotions about the topic, in the end, they were all on board. After much prayer and a season of seeking counsel from others who had walked the adoption road, we pressed forward. We also had the benefit of knowing several other families in our church who had chosen to take the foster-to-adopt route. We didn't take it lightly.

Neither did our adoption agency. We chose to be upfront about our marital struggles with our adoption specialist from day one. He had been a family therapist in previous years, so we weren't sure if that was fortunate or unfortunate for us. As it turned out, he was someone who we couldn't have bluffed even if we had wanted to try, and we learned later that he had drilled down deeper into our history than we thought an adoption agency would. He was exactly who we needed to guide us through the process.

As we committed to move forward, however, there was some flux in our level of relational connection again. Our weekly check-ins had dropped off, the mutual reciprocity for sharing with one another was far from mutual, and the commitments Kevin had made to try new ways to initiate everyday conversations were gone. This throwback to our less-than-intimate past brought with it much emptiness in my heart as I was beginning to envision a family of six. The pause of moving ahead and the Holy Spirit's hesitation stirred within me. Honestly? I wanted to ignore it. I wanted to press on and pretend like it wasn't there. I wanted to blatantly pick up denial. But I had learned in my walk with Jesus that if that nagging sense was ignored, it would only grow stronger. So, I decided to speak up and share what was going on for me.

Kevin was caught a bit off guard. What gives me pause and brings conviction to me are harder for him to notice within himself. He is very quick on his feet with many decisions, but often he has challenges with looking inward—introspection—to examine his perceptions, thoughts, and feelings. This can bring lots of surprises with what seem to be quick transitions.

When I shared my thoughts about adopting with my friend, she urged me to really consider waiting. I didn't want to hear that either. But that's what I truly loved about that friend: she was not afraid to speak hard things into my life, yet I knew she was also praying alongside us for alignment with God's will in this decision.

By this time, I had accepted that there was still more work that God was asking us to do in the area of intimacy in our marriage. Just the thought of that sounded utterly exhausting, but it was also the kick in the backside that we needed. We had come too far to just settle. "Don't just settle" became a running theme. We listened to what God said to us and through others, and then made the call: We would put our adoption plans on hold for a bit. But the hardest part was the seemingly small step of asking the agency to put our adoption file on hold. Well, turns out the agency said they would need to close the file. They explained that they don't put files on hold. My heart sank just hearing those words. That was crushing news, it felt so permanent, like the door closed at that very moment.

When I sought God's guidance, He most often answered, "Yes," "No," "Not now," or "Not yet." I don't claim to know what all the answers to my questions are with God, but when I live in the present moment there is often never a complete "No" unless my request proves to be against His Will. How could adoption, I reasoned, not be God's will? Did not the psalmist say, *"Lord, you know the hopes of the helpless. Surely you will hear their cries and comfort them. You will bring justice to the orphans and the oppressed, so people can no longer terrify them," Psalm 10:17–18.* I kept that verse close to my heart and on a sticky note in the kitchen so I could see it and remember to continually pray for His Will and our direction.

During this time of continued seeking in our marriage, I clung to the hope that God would lead us back to adoption. But now, looking back, I believe that door needed to close completely, allowing us to focus on our marriage, the priority to which God was calling us. It makes sense now why we were not to ignore the promptings.

Although months had stretched to years as we had worked toward intimacy and closer connection in our marriage, God had been clear: we faced more work. Would we obey? Obedience is said to be "the act or practice of obeying; dutiful or submissive compliance,"[1] but how many times in life do we say something to the effect of *"Yes, Lord, I will follow you, but first let me ...."* Luke 9:61. So often we find ourselves being asked by God to go one direction or another, but we have a reason why we should go our own way. We come right to where God wants us, and instead of staying right there and enduring the testing, we turn from it and sometimes even run from it. We don't want to walk the way He's directing, but in those places of closed doors, we grow the most in our submission, not because we aren't getting what we wanted but because we chose to follow the One who knows, absolutely and completely, what is best for us. It stretches us, grows us into completeness, and doesn't allow us to cut corners. I didn't know it then, but if we hadn't faced this challenge and chosen to obey when that door to adoption closed, we would have missed out on so much.

We took the time we needed to repair our relationship over the course of four months and then opened a new file with the adoption agency in early 2016, after much discussion and some grilling from our adoption specialist. And rightfully so: He was standing in for those in our state foster care system who deserve to be in a strong nurturing family. It was abundantly clear that in his prior work as a therapist he had acquired the skill set necessary to do his job. We shared about our recent journey back to intimacy in our marriage—the "work" that, for us, would be lifelong, but we truly felt God's peace leading us back to the agency after empowering us with a deeper connection and concern for this delicate and intimate place in our hearts.

As we moved through the process, we attended adoption classes and completed endless paperwork. By comparison, having a child through natural birth had required only a few pieces of paper and signatures. Even the documentation required for purchasing a house couldn't compare. The adoption process with our agency required not only a truly incredible amount of paperwork but also much "heart" work—mentally, physically, emotionally, and spiritually. The process was unbelievably thorough, but I believe God smiles at the diligence of such agencies when it comes to His little ones.

With the birth of each of our biological kids, we had played a game as an extended family where everyone tried to guess the weight, height, time of birth, etc., before they were born. Needless to say, that wasn't an option with a child in foster care, so we decided to put a jar out on the kitchen counter, and each of us would try to guess the name of the foster child we would soon meet. I asked the kids and Kevin to participate if *God* gave them the name they thought she would have when she came to us. Our then 11-year-old son really got into it and put in names like Deborah, Samantha, and a few others. I reminded him it was names that God led us to, not just any names we thought of, but he just had fun with it.

One morning, a few days later, I had plans to meet with a friend who had adopted three boys. It was a Sunday morning, and we met for coffee. I told her about a dream I'd had the night before we met, and she encouraged me to write it down. It was a very vivid dream: We were to adopt a little girl who was seven years old. She was at a location that functioned as an emergency foster placement center for the state's child protective services department—not a typical source for adoption placement. In my dream, they referred to this little girl as Lorna, and as we were gathering her stuff to leave, they said "We call her Lorna, but her name is Mia." Those details and God's clear vision in my dream were nothing I had experienced before. So, "Mia" was the last name that went in the jar.

Ten days later, on May 3rd, a Tuesday, I was exchanging emails with the director of the Department of Child Services Placement Center, where I volunteered, regarding a personal matter about vacationing. I typed this in at the bottom of the email I was working on: "P.S. Let us know if you hear of a 4-6-year-old sweet girl. We have a bed and room, open and ready."

We were nearly fully certified and approved to adopt and had been assigned a caseworker. We had also just moved our age-range request from five-to-eight years old to four-to-six, because our daughter, Katelyn (nine years old at that time), had been direct and clear that a seven- or eight-year-old sister was too close in age. Within an hour of sending the email, I got a reply: "I might have a 4-year-old for you. Is your certification complete?" I answered that our certification was complete on our end yet was still in process with the court. We were told we could take a child in, even though it could be a while until we received our certification. Within an hour, the director replied, "I have a kid for you. What is your caseworker's name?"

What a completely surreal experience! I immediately forwarded that information to our caseworker, but we didn't hear anything the rest of that day or the whole next day. I did my best to sit on my hands and not send an email each hour (that might have gotten a little obnoxious).

On day three, I finally sent an email to our caseworker telling her we had been talking with the director about a kiddo they might have for us. Then, with one ping on my email, we received a two-page document that had a single picture of our little girl, very minimal information about her and a few other paragraphs, noting that they were looking for a new foster home for her, yet she was with the adoption unit as well.

Her name was Mia.

I was shocked. I could hardly believe it. Then I had a strong, undeniable sense that God was in the depths of this story. My soul had needed encouragement, and now, it was undeniably Him who had given me that dream.

Looking back, I delight in God's humor. When we got that ping on the email, I had just pulled into a parking spot right in front of my dentist's office for a scheduled cleaning. I suppose He knew I just needed to rest for a minute, or better yet about 45 minutes, without much chance to talk, while so much raced through my mind. This wait was welcomed (unlike the other long waits in my marriage) and allowed me to practice my persistence in waiting.

Teeth clean, I raced out and called Kevin right away. We needed further information and to share that we were interested in moving forward. While the emails continued to go back and forth, we spent the weekend writing questions—four pages, double-spaced—that we had about Mia. Within a few days of those initial emails, we had made several phone calls and then had a meeting the next Monday, May 9th, 2016, to ask our questions and for the agency to ask questions of us. A few hours later, we decided we wanted to meet her.

On May 11th, Kevin and I woke knowing we would meet our new daughter that day. As he went about his workday before our meeting, I sat with nervous expectancy at home. It was as if I had been pregnant for so long yet didn't know if I would ever have a baby. Deep within, I was calm, but my surface feelings wanted to take over. For much of my life, I'd kept my feelings in check publicly, especially when events had me expectant and excited. A part of me had always whispered: *Don't get too excited. Keep your emotions in their rightful place. Don't let them consume you.* Yet on this day, I felt like I would burst with anticipation. I nearly walked out of a store, at one point, with a large bed comforter in my hand without paying for it. The cashier kindly asked if she could help me before the obnoxiously loud sensor alarm went off. Thankfully, she may have had some sense that no one in her right mind would try to steal a bed comforter with a ginormous sensor on the outside. It certainly wasn't concealed. I guess you could say I was quite distracted.

That afternoon, I spent time with God in prayer—grateful that I hadn't stolen the bed comforter. Even though there was a deep settling in my soul, my mind was like a pinball machine. The questions kept whirling around: Had I heard Him accurately? Was this fully His will? Did He have this plan set in time long ago? How could I know for sure I was to be her mom? Could I support her well enough to meet her needs? With each question, I did my best to rest in His devoted comfort. He was already sharing with me the answer: *Yes, Shawna, you don't need to make the decision based on your own observation or feelings, but I have already made the decision for you. I even gave you a dream with your little girl's name.*

We arrived at a neutral location, a Barnes and Noble bookstore on the west side of Phoenix, to meet our little girl. As she walked up, I turned to Kevin and said, tearfully, under my breath "She's a doll." I wasn't quite expecting to cry at that moment, so I pulled it together and took a few deep breaths. As we spent time together, she reluctantly opened up to us. We had a sweet, sweet time together, and as we parted, she gave us high fives. We didn't know what every day was going to look like moving forward, but what we did know was our adoption specialist would be our first phone call. Our answer was absolutely *yes!*

The adoption process had been unique, a big step beyond anything we had ever experienced before, but one so worth taking. Just as we had gone through great grief in our marriage for so many years, so had she, with unfulfilled longings for her birth family. We had in common our need for connection, and the enduring trials we had all been through to this point were not far from our hearts. Mia, we believed, would someday know that both our story and hers had been divinely orchestrated by her loving Savior.

That first week was one we will never forget. She and the kids bonded quickly. She called our oldest "big brudder," Katelyn was "widdle gurl," and Tyler, her "udder brudder." You can imagine the chuckles as she named them all before she learned their real names. Tyler was a good sport about "udder" brother— that four-year-old's pronunciation gave us a good laugh. Even today, as a preteen, she still loves to hear this story.

We had a nice, ten-day honeymoon period with Mia, as we got to know her, and she got to know us. Ten days was better than some stories we had heard, so we were somewhat aware that a new reality would eventually set in. When it did, there was a lot to work through with Mia. Four years and nine months of age when she joined our family, Mia had been in foster care since she was two-and-a-half, and we were her fourth foster placement. She'd also been moved from place to place before she was permanently removed from her birth-mom's care. She'd had neither stability nor consistency in her short life, so we wondered if she could truly attach to us. One of my greatest fears was that my little girl would have been through so much by this age that her brain and body would not allow her to attach securely to me. We were determined to do all we could to help her as best we could. It wasn't long before we learned that she did know how to attach, despite trauma causing disorganization in her brain from an early age. I recognized that her attachment struggle was similar to what I had experienced in my marriage, time and time again.

We were challenged as parents, as a couple, and as a family. We had never experienced the extreme emotional dysregulation in our other kids at this level. We knew that Mia had been removed from her previous placement because of her behaviors, and we knew a bit of what we had signed up for from a few red flags on that initial two-page document. We learned pretty quickly we would need to lean on God and on each other a lot during this process. It was going to be one day at a time and, sometimes, one minute at a time.

Mia lacked the skills to control her emotions and organize them in a way that made sense. This is common for kids in foster care. Some foster kids show this disorganization and lack of control outwardly in the form of anger and rage. In Mia, it was extreme, and we learned that her brain was operating primarily from her limbic system, the place of fight or flight. Said to be the "smoke detector" of the brain, it can't tell the difference between real and perceived threats. She was hypervigilant, wanting to gain control as best she could, a strategy that often backfired. Calming herself and slowing down was not yet part of what she knew how to do. We had a long way to go, and we needed help.

Thankfully, we'd become comfortable with therapy in our family, and we chose to continue with external help for trauma therapy and later added occupational and equine therapy. Much later, we realized she had ADHD and anxiety. Our commitments for her care and support were significant.

Her emotions could be overpowering. Her demand for autonomy and finding her place in the family at a young age was confusing for us. There were tears and screams from her on many occasions, not to mention tears from almost all the rest of us in the family at times. There were times we found ourselves staying in parking lots for extended periods to wait for the *stormies* (what we called her tantrums) to pass before we could enter our destination.

We invited God to heal her little body and provide us with His strength to make it through the exhausting moments, emotionally and physically. I vividly remember the time when the five of us were on our knees outside of her room praying to the Lord for His healing and presence, while she was inside the room screaming, "Don't pray for me!" We felt helpless in a human sense.

We've spent hours, and sometimes days, recalling what we could do differently to help her, how we felt bad for how we had reacted, what we could do to change things next time, and how we could all grow from an experience. It has been the hardest parenting that we have experienced thus far, and we found comfort in taking what God had taught us through our marriage and using it to help Mia heal. We were and are determined for more for her, too. She, in turn, showed us in her tiny body what we were both healing from in the years prior. "Being able to feel safe with other people is probably the single most important aspect of mental health; safe connections are fundamental to meaningful and satisfying lives."[2]

———

Trauma recovery in both of our adult lives had mended scars that we experienced, and to see abandonment through the lens of a child whose pain we didn't cause, couldn't control, and certainly couldn't cure on our own, was an extremely complex experience. Despite all the heartache she had to go through to get to us, we are so very grateful for her story. It has allowed us to see how far we have come, personally, and what we had to offer her in the process. We wouldn't have Mia if we had pushed through when He nudged us to wait. In my dream that revealed her name, our certification timing, and our first meeting with her, it's clear that God had a plan all along.

Our prayer from the beginning has been to let us be to her what she'd never experienced and to let her bring to us a love for her that we've never quite felt before. We believe God has healed and will continue to heal our little girl. So we wait. We wait, and wait, and wait some more, with Holy anticipation, to see how she will use the gift of healing in her own life.

CHAPTER 20

Embracing Recovery

With the eclectic array of dimensions to our history, we made a commitment to see a specialist in late 2016. We didn't want to lose anything we had already gained, and we were willing to try for more. We had a few phone calls with her to assess the fit, and over a few months of prayer, we decided to take a leap financially and commit to a three-day intensive in Texas, just outside of Dallas. Kevin's corporate office was there, so he felt this could be a good fit for potential follow-up visits. We both tried our best to go in with palms up and open hearts to allow God to dig deeper and get those deeper layers into the light. Although I knew this was the best next step, I still felt uncertainty and nervousness, especially on the plane ride there. Apprehension and hope were held in tension. When we arrived, my chest was tight, and I imagined Kevin's was, too. As we walked into the specialist's office, I noticed a lump in my throat. My body felt lethargic before we even began.

An hour or so into our first session, however, we relaxed, kicked off our shoes, covered up with a blanket, and got comfortable with one another. We didn't waste any time letting her see our spiral and how fast we could get there. We had done this therapy thing many times before, and we knew that the sooner we started talking and not holding up a mask of deception, the sooner we could get somewhere. Much to our surprise, she quickly separated us for some individual work. I don't know if this was her normal strategy, but she began untangling what I believe were those remaining strings of our dysfunction that were still knotted up.

Kevin went off to do some assessment work to determine his specific area of sexual addiction and love addiction/love avoidance. We hadn't ever looked at this before because his infidelity hadn't been an issue for more than eight years by this point. The assessment confirmed that he had a process addiction of sorts, seeking love from others versus a form of sexual addiction that was more chemically driven. We had read online that there were different forms of sexual addiction, but this came together in her words better than we had been able to determine through our own research, and less-than-professional discussions at home.

I worked with the therapist on how complex trauma that she identified from my early years had carried over into our marriage. It was incredibly eye-opening to me and made sense. No wonder things got so tangled up! Those traumatic memories could get triggered quickly, and I couldn't dodge them. My body would just react. I had to find what I needed in a given moment to regulate my body and bring emotional safety and mental sanity to my reality. Most importantly, I had to do so out of my own internal strength, instead of looking to Kevin to help bring calm to my body, which he often wasn't able to provide.

Toward that end, I began therapeutic trauma-healing work with her that day, and as she prompted me, I found imagery for my safe place: a serene creek. I named my place, *Easy to Find Joy.* I had always loved creeks. If you gave me the choice to visit a creek in the woods or a beautiful tropical ocean, I would pick a creek any day. Such a scene had always brought me peace, and now, I was able to create it for future reference during tough moments. My creek had really cold water, nestled against a tall, wild, brushy hillside. Up on the hill was a deer—in biblical symbolism, that can mean longing and aspiration—that often watched over me. The water was moving but not fast. It came up to my mid-calf. The rocks were smooth to walk on, and there was a raft nearby, should the water rise. The temperature outside was in the mid-70s, and there was a faint color of purple in the air. Once created, it was easy to get to, and it was my place. No one could take it away. I had a team there with me, and I could call on them all. My circle of safe people was often hand-in-hand with me. Jesus was right there standing in the water with me, and when I would turn, his hand would often be upon me. My creek was peaceful, and I frequented it a lot during those days in her office. Even writing about it now brings me a soothing sense of peace and reminds me that I'll always have a place of retreat.

⁓

Another amazing exercise I did while there was writing who I was. Over the years, I had maintained some false core beliefs about myself. Those beliefs were the ugly roots of my poor reactions and decision-making. Some were longstanding and had begun to dissolve. Some were still there, and this helped replace them. An actual statement of who I was gave me strength in the toughest of times was a form of self-love, a map for my heart. I share it here, not to boast, but as a testimony of the hope and strength it brought me:

> *I am not mean, but I can act mean. I am a fighter, for the things that matter most to me. I consider my responsibilities a priority. I appreciate consistency. I am an honest person who desires honest relationships. I value authenticity in others. I'm willing to be vulnerable. I risk even when I may not feel completely safe. I will set boundaries to protect myself and my heart. I am reasonable. I am consistent in my words and actions. What I say and how I treat others matters to me. I feel remorse when I have hurt someone. I give chances to rebuild trust. I take people at their word. I like that I persevere and don't give up. I don't have to be right. I forgive and offer grace. I hold stress in my neck and jaw. I can be aware of my body. I can be critical and judgmental and strive to be more compassionate and grateful. I don't have to be over-responsible. I don't have to react but am learning to respond. I can love and be loved.*

I knew that I would be all right with or without Kevin close to me. Whether for a moment, a day, a year, or a lifetime, I could choose not to accept harmful behavior. I could walk away and take care of myself. I began to see myself differently. To cherish myself. Not allowing, and I mean truly for the first time, not allowing other people's moods or comments to sting like they had before. I took responsibility for joy in each of my days. I felt like a delicate Christmas ornament at times—something to protect from damage, something to be cared for tenderly.

Then, there was *sensuality*. Maybe you can imagine the looks on our faces when our therapist introduced this to us: Eyes averted, heads lowered, shoulders slumped. I'm sure we aren't the only ones who have responded that way—at least, I have to hope. The word, sensuality, itself was foreign to both Kevin and me. While I find myself a little nerdy and preoccupied with the dictionary sometimes, I looked up "sensual," and one definition read "devoted to or preoccupied with the senses or appetites."[1] What followed was a learning experience that was especially uncomfortable because the therapist was sitting there watching us, as she had us practice taking slow steps toward sensuality. I love her for it now, but I wanted to go running out of the room when she asked me to participate.

As we learned to look deeply into each other's eyes, embrace each other without focusing on the end result of sex, and move toward each other in a more intentional way, I did my best. I truly did. But at the beginning, I would just sort of fall into this awkward laughter, a chuckle—not really sure what to call it. Here I was, a 42-year-old mother of four, giggling like a 13 year-old teenager. But though we had to restart a few times because I had a smirk on my face out of embarrassment, I did participate. I embraced my embarrassment and uncomfortable feelings and, all joking aside, it truly provided a new level of connection for us.

I was sharing this concept with a newly married friend who struggled sexually with her husband of just a few weeks, and she nearly rejected it at first, but later came back to tell me how much it helped. I truly wish sensual awareness was a part of our culture. Maybe then, sexualized behavior wouldn't be the focus, and our needs would be met and respected because we would all learn how to connect in love *without* all the taboos and wrong thinking about our own sexuality. For this reason, I appreciated the opportunity to share my experience. Although my stomach was in knots as I wrote about this topic, I also desired that my hopes for my continued journey sexually might be realized as well. And some of them have! It's much more enjoyable now. Who would have thought?!

Shortly after we finished our first few hours of sharing on day one, the therapist decided that we *both* needed to do some EMDR work to reduce the noise in our brains that tended to elevate our current struggles. Quieting the noise in my brain from the past made a lot of sense to me as I thought about current situations. Some of this noise came from way back in childhood. It wasn't always my present reality, but somehow, my brain thought that noise was helpful in my current situation. I learned that my body needed some much deeper healing that I couldn't do on my own. The effects of Complex Post Traumatic Stress Disorder (C-PTSD) were notable, and I needed to continue to seek help and support from others and ultimately the One who heals. Jesus had shown up and done mighty work in my life thus far, and I expected no less now. I was willing to walk toward further healing with the Lord, and it was worth it. During this continued EMDR work in therapy, I believe God has transformed my mind by allowing it the capacity to perceive differently. I felt as if God had removed the old debris that wasn't meant to be there. He had not only removed it but had also restored it with what He wanted to put in its place.

Traumatic responses and their effects aren't a walk in the

park, to say the least. They are real, bold, and sometimes debilitating. They can take you down when you least expect it. I had come to a place where I listened to my body better, and I didn't want to abandon the temple that the Lord had given me anymore. The Apostle Paul pleads with us in Romans 12:1-2, *"Give your bodies to God. Let them be a living and holy sacrifice—the kind he will accept. When you think of what he has done for you, is this too much to ask? Don't copy the behavior and customs of this world, but let God transform you into a new person by changing the way you think. Then you will know what God wants you to do, and you will know how good and pleasing and perfect his will really is."*

This renewing of the mind can be done in both conscious and unconscious thinking. "Mind: The Greek word is *nous* which views the mind as the capacity to perceive. We're no longer to look at life's issues as mere human beings, but let our perceptions be reshaped by God's own revelation of reality in the Scriptures."[2]

A lot happened in those 20 hours of therapy. Yes, 20 whole hours! For the first time, I was perfectly content to exchange only a few words with Kevin on the flight home. We were utterly exhausted. But I had learned that I could believe new truths, not the "truths" about myself I had received from others, but those shaped by God Himself. I had also realized that I can withstand what life brings by keeping my reality in balance. Kevin had begun to determine his inherent worth, and I could continue to pray for him. He still had moments of deflecting responsibility, but I didn't have to accept it in a harmful way. I could be cherished in a new and different way now. I am thankful for that essential time away and all that we gained. Growth, stillness, a rest from within.

CHAPTER 21

Stones for our Altar

Shortly after we arrived home, I decided that, along with the work we were doing together, I was going to continue with my still unmet goal of reading through the Bible, cover to cover, for the first time. I had attempted this before on a few occasions, but I'd never made it very far. When I arrived back home, I was in the book of Joshua:

> *When all the people had crossed the Jordan, the Lord said to Joshua, "Now choose twelve men, one from each tribe. Tell them to take twelve stones from where the priests are standing in the middle of the Jordan and pile them up at the place where you camp tonight. So, Joshua called together the twelve men and told them, 'Go into the middle of the Jordan, in front of the Ark of the Lord your God. Each of you must pick up one stone and carry it out on your shoulder—twelve stones in all, one for each of the twelve tribes. We will use these stones to build a memorial. In the future, your children will ask, 'What do these stones mean to you?' Then you can tell them, 'They remind us that the Jordan River stopped flowing when the Ark of the Lord's Covenant went across.' These stones will stand as a permanent memorial among the*

people of Israel." So, the men did as Joshua had commanded them. They took twelve stones from the middle of the Jordan River, one for each tribe, just as the Lord had told Joshua. They carried them to the place where they camped for the night and constructed the memorial there. Joshua also built another memorial of twelve stones in the middle of the Jordan, at the place where the priests who carried the Ark of the Covenant were standing. The memorial remains there to this day (Joshua 4:2-9).

I had come home wanting to focus on gratitude and appreciation, despite my circumstances, choosing some new strategies in this spiritual battle. That's who I wanted to be. As I read Joshua 4, I felt gratitude for the unfathomable intimacy that God showed me that very morning. Today, this story in Joshua is different and powerful. This is what I wrote in my journal, with tears streaming down my face: *As I remain in the hope that God can and will bring recovery and healing, I accept my desire to be cherished and adored by Kevin. I must die to the dream of what that will look like. The desire is built within me, but in the unfolding, I choose to look to God to show me through all the small stones, the miracles.*

Joshua speaks of the Israelites wandering for forty years in the wilderness, yet God was faithful in their disobedience. Our story has been many years of uncertainty, confusion, and fighting to be cherished, in a wilderness of our own where God has been faithful in our wandering.

God promised to lead them to a land more fruitful than their hopes and richer than their dreams. Our story was God's promise of a marriage far more rewarding than we could ever ask for or imagine. God came to show His love to us.

The pivotal moment for the Israelites was when they were ready to enter the Promised Land only to find the Jordan at flood levels, fast and dangerous. It was impassible, its crossing impossible. Our story had brought us to the flood waters as we entered intensive counseling in Texas, realizing the depths and dangers of our intimacy and attachment issues.

Then God rolled back the chaotic waters in the Jordan and instructed Joshua to take 12 stones from the dry riverbed. Our story was about God bringing us to greater acceptance of our dry land. Asking me to take the stones from the dry middle of the road of our healing. God had made a way.

God calmed the waters. Rages stopped flowing in the living presence of God so they could do their part of picking up the stones. Our story was the Holy Spirit's presence in our parallel tale, weaving into our hearts and minds that God can calm any raging flood at any moment.

In obedience, Joshua picked up the stones and built an altar. Symbolic acts that helped God's people identify with a work of God on their behalf. In our story, I was to go out and cherish those moments of connection each day. Taking a stone and placing it in a clear fragile vase, in our place of rest, our bedroom, as a reminder of what He had done.

Remembering the Promised Land was a place of battle. A place of trust. Challenges got bigger but so did the blessings. Our story was our battleground. Remembering our battle had not been won, yet also remembering God's faithfulness. The challenges did get bigger, but we trusted that the blessing would, too. This was the both-and.

Then Joshua said to the Israelites, "In the future, your children will ask, 'What do these stones mean?' Then you can tell them, 'This is where the Israelites crossed the Jordan on dry ground.' For the Lord your God dried up the river right before your eyes, and he kept it dry until you were all across, just as he did at the Red Sea when he dried it up until we had all crossed over. He did this so all the nations of the earth might know the power of the Lord, and that you might fear the Lord your God forever." Joshua 4:21-24

That vase still sits on my bookcase, for our children and future grandchildren to see. Each stone I placed is a reminder of God's faithful provision of a simple hug, a kiss, a kind word, an apology, a prayer, a show of compassion, a sweet gesture, an encouragement. I put stones in that vase not only for the big things that I saw but also for the small things. Those small miracles have been added to hundreds of others that show the powerful hand of the One I stand before in reverent awe. In a small yet significant side note, the journal that I picked up to write that day had been sitting in my bookcase for some time and was titled *Be Filled with Joy.*

"Don't be dejected and sad, for the joy of the Lord is your strength," Nehemiah 8:10.

Truly, His joy is far beyond the sheer happiness of big things. Finding joy in the simple, small things is what has truly opened my eyes.

Here's one more journal entry—a glimpse of life as I embraced the small miracles:

Oh, what a week it has been. It had been 2 1/2 months since we went to our intensive in Texas. Progress has been made and I'm learning to listen to my body. Helping get it regulated sooner with the boundaries I have set. The breathing, making lots of calls and going to my place are often "easy to find joy." I have been focusing on my values. Calm and emotionally secure within God and myself first and then shifting my thinking to gratitude. Honoring myself and learning to listen to what is right for me. Allowing myself to grieve when I need to. I still have the desire within me to be pursued. I always will. God built that in me. Dying to the dream of how and when I will be cherished and what that looks like. Truly it's God's timing for me, if on this earth, and Kevin's choice and obedience to true healing. Such a place of deep sorrow yet acceptance and surrender of what it can be. Choosing to watch and see the small miracle of Kevin's pursuit of me. Writing a gratitude list each day of the ways I am pursued. Putting a stone in my tall and fragile vase next to the place I sleep. Writing it out in my "filled with joy" journal. I've surrendered to my fight to be pushing for pursuit of me. I cannot lead this marriage. I am finally learning to follow despite being led. Kevin is trying to move into intimacy though often being pulled back with fear and resistance. My focus for now is to take good care of myself, especially focusing on my health concerns. It's been hard to put self-protection and anger down. I have felt much of the deprivation and trauma wounds fully now. No matter what, I want to be fully present with myself. Remembering what I really need from this moment. Keeping my heart open and not resisting when Kevin does move close. Lord, may I walk in your ways in reality and may we have a marriage built on a foundation of love and truth and joy.

There was a specific incident in early 2017, when I realized, finally, that I needed to put down my old self-protecting anger and feel the trauma and emotional deprivation wounds. I had gone into a full-blown trauma reaction. At that moment, I knew that my husband's spiritual strongholds were out trying to coerce him to protect himself, saying to me, "Get the heck away from me." I lost my ability to continue with my morning because of Kevin's destructive demeanor. My body began shaking and I bit the tip of my thumb as I asked him to please take our daughter to school. After shakily making my way upstairs, I began crying, and I found it difficult to breathe. Alone, I began rocking to soothe myself, similar to how an infant is soothed by an attentive mother. I repeated over and over to myself, "I'm ok, I'm ok, I'm ok ...."

After allowing the depths of the sorrow to surface, I took deep breaths, took a shower, and shuttled our younger daughter to preschool. Shortly after coming home for a nap at 8:30 a.m., I began to recognize my response for what it was: This trauma had often been there, but my body was finally feeling its full effects because other, less helpful coping strategies weren't in use anymore. The deprivation that had been set aside came front and center, and I could feel *everything*. Now, however, I knew how to self-soothe without pressing forward, and what an immense step forward for my physical and emotional health it was! After that day, I knew that I wanted to be absolutely present with myself. Remembering what I really needed in that moment and then choosing it was my greatest strength.

PART III

Trusting in the Purpose

"Though the Lord gave you adversity ... he will still be with you. You will see your teacher with your own eyes, and you will hear a voice say, 'This is the way; turn around and walk here.'"
Isaiah 30:20-21

CHAPTER 22

_____

Sharing with The Kids

Trust and authenticity with our kids have always been important to Kevin and me. For my part, I wanted to provide them, as they grew up, a secure, trusting relationship that would remain so as they stepped into adulthood. Our journey had been tough on me as a mom because I had to do my very best to protect my own heart and well-being so that I could be there to do the same for our kids. There were moments I felt like a rock star, guarding the hearts of my kids from any sense of responsibility for our marital struggle, but other times I felt like a complete wreck and failure, saying and doing things that I regretted—allowing them to hear yelling, slammed doors, and see my desperate tears. This sometimes left them with a sense of helplessness and worry. They knew our relationship had conflict, and I wondered how much they should have seen and heard. We tried our best to show repair when it was possible but sometimes failed to do so.

In addition to the common conflicts, I realized early on that, one day, our kids would need to hear our story. We'd been through the betrayal and the preceding divorce, and I desperately didn't want family secrets. Sometimes, I imagined Kevin being forced to tell them all he had done, me not caring if he would feel shame or embarrassment. I would play the injustice over and over in my head. He was going to tell them whether he liked it or not, and I wasn't too concerned for his comfort. That was one of the uglier sides of me. Other times, my internal thought process was a little softer, focusing on what would be best for the kids and striving to not put them in the middle of the mess.

I imagined we would sit down with our kids together, and I would allow Kevin to share with them his behaviors, and I would share my experience. Because our kids were so young when the affairs happened and our recovery as a couple was at the forefront in the years that followed, I knew the time was not yet right for sharing. So, I did my best to put that on a shelf and work on my healing. I knew that I needed to be strong for them even if they became upset with me or thought I caused it somehow. Through the years, I prayed that God would make it clear when and how He would have us share with them. If I could help it, I didn't want them carrying any burden for our relationship.

But when it comes to disclosures to kids, there are times when one doesn't have the luxury to wait. I completely grieve with those mamas who have to tell much of the story to their kids because they heard or suspected something or witnessed confrontations or a lack of recovery that led to an out-of-house separation or divorce. It just breaks my heart and makes me mad that betrayed wives and betrayed husbands have to heal while simultaneously holding the emotions and broken hearts of many little humans. It feels unfair, and yet I give so much credit to those who do it and support their kids so well.

Ideally, when the time for full disclosure came, we desired our children to have their own, individual support from a therapist who understands child mental health and stages of development. That desire wasn't a reality for them all but that was our goal. Kids' brains develop differently, based on their age, emotional maturity, and lived circumstances. We do our best as parents most of the time, but we don't know what we don't know. I know I am still learning.

That said, when our family disclosure process actually began to unfold, we were "winging it" a lot, doing what we thought would be best for them and then praying. Connor, our oldest, who had gone through the divorce and remarriage with us, was and still is a wise young man with a strong sense of who he is. When we did full disclosure with him, he was 17 years old, and already firmly believed that God was real and was for him.

It began when he and Kevin went on a men's retreat together in 2017, just about eight years to the day since Kevin had first shared his deceptive acting out behavior. We had not planned to initiate disclosure at the retreat, but once Kevin was on that mountain, at the retreat, he felt a gentle nudge from God to share his story with Connor. He did reach out to ask me if I was okay with that. Given the circumstances, I went with it: we had already talked through, thoroughly, what we would say when we did disclose, and I believed he had Connor's best interests at heart. I would not have been okay if Kevin had done it to get something off his chest or if he was just trying to "get it over with." But I truly felt he was listening to and obeying God, and I certainly didn't want to get in the way.

Nevertheless, I sat with sweaty palms and a racing heart during the time when they would be talking. I prayed, asking God to fill in any spaces of confusion for Connor, then I waited. I felt honored when Kevin chose to let me know how the conversation had gone. Although I had been fearful he would be hurt by the disclosure, I really didn't fear the ultimate outcome for Connor. His tender soul had, in fact, taken it all in, and he had told Kevin thoughtfully, "Now, it's time to rewrite this story." Could you imagine what a relief that was for Kevin and me? Our sweet little boy, who had been through so much, had shared this wisdom with the dad who had fractured our family. I felt so proud.

Although the other kids were still too young for full disclosure, God was busy disclosing the new direction I was to take. As I listened to the stirrings within me in the Spring of 2018, I realized that God was asking me to take a completely different career direction, one that would use our story to provide strength to others. Our marriage was much more stable at that point, and I was ready to take all I had learned and use it for the good of others. So, I prayed, and I waited until I heard clearly that next step: I was to become a specialized betrayal trauma coach in order to share my experience and hope with others who were walking through similar journeys.

Remember when I said that I have self-diagnosed phonemic awareness dyslexia? I sought the best certified coaching program I could find, and despite my challenges, I focused on this for the next few years, while simultaneously obtaining specialized training and certification through APSATS, the Association of

Partners of Sex Addicts Trauma Specialists [1]. APSATS offers a treatment model which shifts the outdated perspective of codependency to the more accurate perspective of partners experiencing trauma—a far cry from what I was offered in my early recovery journey. I eventually opened my private practice and began writing what would eventually become this book. With four kids at home, ranging in age from 6 to 18, I stayed busy!

In 2020 and 2021, respectively, we shared our story with our two middle kiddos: Tyler at age 15 and Katelyn at age 14. These two kids were younger when we disclosed this because we had become increasingly more confident in our ability to share appropriately and were more aware of our children's need to understand what the previous devastation of our family life had been. As he had with Connor, Kevin shared with Tyler alone, then I had the opportunity, shortly afterward, to have a fill-in-the-blank conversation about my experience. The solo disclosure from his dad was due to the timing of a few circumstances, but it was clear, nevertheless, that God had asked us to share with him in that time frame. My sweet, bouncy baby boy, who I had nicknamed Tigger, was now as tall as I was, and still growing. He listened intently, heard, and took in every word, and, like Connor before him, he was mature and caring in his response. The same kid who had run and hidden behind the shower curtain when we first talked to him about sex, was all grown up. It blew me away.

Sharing with Katelyn was tougher for Kevin. She was his little girl. I knew I wanted to be present when we did disclosure with the girls to ensure that it wasn't just a guy-to-guy chat, but rather, a time for us to have an authentic, genuine conversation about all that had happened. Although Katelyn was a year younger than Tyler when we shared, she was close to Tyler, emotionally and socially. We wanted to disclose our history to both of them, so they each had a safe person to talk it out with. There was a little space in between but Tyler did not share it with his sister before we shared it with her.

This was the first time I had the initial conversation with any of them. The three of us sat on our L-shaped couch with Katelyn in the middle looking back and forth as we each told pieces of the story at an age-appropriate level without details or non-pertinent information. She took it all in. She is our internal processor, and that was evident during the conversation. She looked at me for much of the time to see how I was responding. When she heard about the affairs, specifically, and how much Dad had hurt Mom, she began to cry. Her ability to hold this information for herself yet stay attuned to me was a source of tender moments I would long remember.

That said, I wanted to make sure she knew that it wasn't her responsibility to make sure I was alright. Instead, it was my job to make sure she was alright. This was no small matter. Kids often try to fill roles in a family by determining intuitively where the greatest need is and then attempting to meet it. It was so important to me that she not take on more than her own needs. I deeply desired for her heart to hear, process, and grieve the reality of her family history as needed.

Our last kiddo to know was our Mia-Mia. That soul of hers had the maturity of a thirty-year-old at times, and that of a three-year-old at other times. Such is the effect of early childhood trauma and neglect. Parts of her had needed to grow up fast to survive, while other parts of her cried out for the safe haven and secure base of her biological mom who, sadly, wasn't able to meet those needs consistently.

We chose to disclose to Mia in 2022, at the age of 11. This was much earlier than I ever imagined telling any of our kids, especially considering that Connor was only nine-years-old when Kevin's infidelity and the events its discovery triggered originally took place. We had said, early on, that once, or if, we decided to share our story publicly, we wanted to make sure that we had shared it with our kids first, and that they had a voice and a choice if we did share publicly. If they were ever uncomfortable with that process, we wanted to pause and support their needs first. This is one of the main reasons we had tried our very best to keep our story under tight wraps until this point.

We made our best attempt to keep it at an elementary-school level—Mia was still in fifth grade—yet also state the facts and acknowledge the truth. Our intuitive Mia took it all in stride, and she asked questions that were deep and wide. We knew that her questions would surpass, in depth, the questions asked by her three siblings combined.

She asked, and she asked some more. She really does have a feral curiosity, and that is coupled with unbounded empathy, earned through soul-breaking lived experiences. We wanted her to feel a sense of safety and security in our time together. But she asked questions that, I hoped, didn't reveal my surprise and terror on the inside.

With eyes open almost as big as the frames of her little round glasses, she got her answers. I think they shocked her. When we curbed the questions after several rounds, we told her this didn't need to be our last conversation and that we could talk about this as long as we needed to in years to come. That seemed to suffice, and she was settled. In her innocent and empathetic way, she said, "Thanks for answering my questions and for sharing with me." Oh, my mama heart was filled to the brim with relief that all our kids now knew, and what I knew one day would be told.

I don't ever want to claim these decisions were easy to make or simple to carry out, because there were lots of tears, tenseness, and concern. Yet, the Spirit of God was so ever-present. When we felt there were no words to share, the words came. When we just simply didn't want to have those conversations, the courage was given. When they all knew, we were able to look back and see that His timing was what it needed to be. We accept that, even today, without judging ourselves in hindsight. We will move forward as it comes up and keep checking in with the kids. We want these conversations to be part of an ongoing pattern of transparency for a lifetime.

CHAPTER 23

Filling the Gaps

After years of therapy and hard work, Kevin and I had reached a point where our relationship bore little resemblance to the one that had been stifled with infidelity and had since become the subject of our disclosures to our children. Once almost unable to resist flight on the flight-or-fight scale—especially when I chose to fight—and so prone to fear-driven dishonesty that he might lie to me even when there was nothing to fear, Kevin had worked hard for most of a decade to overcome such habitual relationship sabotage. The result, in many cases, had been exceptional. He'd taken the lead when we'd made our disclosures to Connor and Tyler. That alone had been a triumph for honesty.

Most remarkable, when he was away from home, Kevin was able to "show up" and show genuine empathy when it came to the struggles I had with Mia as her fourth mama. He could sit with me on the phone while she screamed or cried, even when he was on a work trip, traveling to meetings with coworkers or waiting at an airport. Knowing I was no longer alone in parenting when I was alone at home was soothing to my core.

Unfortunately, when he was home with me and I wanted to connect, he could still freeze up. From a distance—checking on me from afar—it had become much easier for him to connect. But often, when he came home from a work trip, he would walk in, ask if the dogs had been fed, read the mail, or even check on something in the yard before asking how I was doing. I'd try to engage in small talk or share about something in my day, and it was as if he was deaf. He would often not respond. And when he did, he'd change the subject.

These moments left me in utter confusion. But I've since come to learn that Kevin suffers severe limitations in his ability to process body language, facial expressions, and other sensory input during verbal communication. This made it incredibly hard for him to communicate effectively in person.

Recently, God has been speaking to me boldly about Kevin's continuing freeze-ups and other issues in two ways. One way is that He often wakes me at night and drops in thoughts that completely resonate with me. Oddly, they make sense but are not my own. It is quite surreal, and I most often know it is God speaking rather than random thoughts because I have peace when I wake, and confusion is absent.

The other way God speaks to me is through visual analogies. One that I remember vividly is an analogy in which my marriage resembles a lake. Sometimes the water is so clear and I am able to see the sunset reflected on its surface. But at other times, the lake is full of algae and unable to reflect the sun's light. I'm trying not to get too far ahead of myself as I'll definitely share more about that with you later. Oh, it was incredibly significant.

Though I can be logical in many areas of my life, God allows for creativity in my thoughts to help me understand what He is saying. I find these to be cherished gifts in the relationship that God and I have built together through the Holy Spirit.

One typical weekday afternoon, as I was standing at the sink, another visual came to mind: When I reach out my cup under a faucet, sometimes there is water. My cup gets filled up, and what it contains quenches my thirst. Other times the water doesn't come. I remain thirsty and can't force the water to come out. Sometimes the faucet is broken. I don't keep waiting under that same faucet demanding that it work or bang on it until the water comes out. The water may turn on again, but until it does, I know that God will quench my every thirst: I can go to the deep well of water out back as often as I need to, hoping the faucet will turn on again, yet knowing I don't need it to survive.

The reality was that sexual betrayal is brutally painful and emotional deprivation can quite honestly be torturous at times, threatening my attachment system. In this visual picture, Kevin was the faucet. Sometimes, water was present and available; at other times, it was not there at all. That all-too-vivid analogy made so much sense. I lived that. It was important that I kept a true sense of reality and accepted this situation for what it was. Kevin had made progress from years past, but there were still times when he was *gone and unavailable*; the faucet was completely dry. I would ask him questions, like "Where did my husband go?" and he would look back at me and say, "What do you mean? I'm right here." I would reply, "It's as if you left and didn't realize I was still standing here," and he'd say, "but I didn't leave." I would often thirst for connection and closeness and would realize the faucet was unavailable at that moment. The toughest part, for me, was deciphering when to stay available for a connection, and when to detach from Kevin's unavailability and get my desire met elsewhere. Although I do believe my husband is being called to be present more of the time, in the faucet analogy, God is always available to fill the void from the deep well of his living water.

⸻

I remember a specific moment talking with God and desiring to understand why He built such a thirst within me for closeness and belonging together, when such intimacy was only available to me sparingly. *Was I really asking too much? Was this desire too great within me? Was I too much? Was this need intended to be filled by Kevin at all?*

God says intimacy is good, and it is a special part of the marriage bond. That's Biblical. But, as we strive for closer emotional, physical, and spiritual intimacy in our marriage, God has His own timing. In the moments of struggle, God might be more concerned with getting my heart right with Him and reminding me through this struggle that He desires to provide for me. I have learned that God is often more concerned with the process than the outcome. The stark reality is that our timeline is not of greatest concern for God.

A good friend once said that when God wants to make a giant oak tree, he takes 100 years, but when he wants to make a mushroom, he does it overnight. It was a keen reminder to be patient in the process if I desired to be a giant oak tree one day.

⸻

Scripturally, I believe God has designed a man and a woman to feel loved and respected mutually. *"So again, I say, each man must love his wife as he loves himself, and the wife must respect her husband"* in Ephesians 5:33 is a great starting point, but it isn't as cut and dried as I was taught. Kevin and I have had lengthy discussions about it, and we looked at it through the lens of our marriage.

For so many years, Kevin sought after love from me and others to fill the void that only God could fill, yet he didn't have the love for himself that Scriptures speak of, the kind of agape love—the highest form of love—from Father God for us. The Lord says:

"Not even a sparrow, worth only half a penny, can fall to the ground without your Father knowing it. And the very hairs on your head are all numbered. So don't be afraid; you are more valuable to him than a whole flock of sparrows,"
Matthew 10:29-31.

Early on, as we began our relationship, I desired respect and to have a man of integrity. I had experienced genuine love in many areas growing up, so that wasn't my primary craving, but respect—being treated kindly, knowing that I was known, sure that I was heard—was lacking. When that was absent in our relationship, I didn't take notice right away. There was criticism and blame received and reciprocated before we were even engaged to be married the first time. Being loved and cherished was often a place too tender for me to go without respect, so my insistence for respect became a defense mechanism. I desired, pushed for, and demanded respect above all else.

I also couldn't fully let my guard down to be respected without safety and trust. Without respect, I couldn't let the love in completely. I have always known Kevin loved me in a general sense even though his actions didn't align with that belief sometimes. Yet I sat at a crossroads of reciprocal love. Giving and receiving are two different dimensions of love, but they are interdependent: We cannot give love to another if we have not yet fully received love. And the only One who can give us an agape love worth passing on to another is God. Until we both received the complete love of our Lord, there was an unbridgeable gap. For a long time, Kevin wasn't able to fully receive my love because he had not yet allowed his Heavenly Father to give him that depth of love. He didn't believe he deserved it. That insecurity was behind the dishonesty and withdrawal that triggered my disrespect and prevented me from receiving the love he tried to give me. Because Kevin had not fully accepted God's love, he could not respect himself, and, therefore, was unable either to accept my love or earn my respect. We both had to get rightly aligned with God first before Ephesians 5:33 even made sense to us.

CHAPTER 24

Trials, Transparency, and Trust

The past has more clarity and certainty because it has been completed. I have reflected more on God's goodness and his restoration of our marriage than anything else because I now understand why God allowed its troubles to come our way. Some parts of our story, however, might never make complete sense in terms of the "why." In fact, I don't think asking "why" was ever really important. It is the "what" that has always been crucial. What are we to do with the circumstances? *What are we to fight for? Fight against? What will we see more clearly through it all? What makes God's plan better than ours?* If I had all the answers for "why," I might fumble more because that question would pull me back into my need for my own understanding and my own need to have certainty about God's Will. I needed to trade trust in my often imperfect understanding for trust in the God who understands perfectly.

A prayer that I wrote and laminated can routinely be found around my house, on my nightstand and in my books and, sometimes, old folders, stands as a strong reminder of this choice:

> *Lord, I have often tried my own ways and do things through*

my own self-sufficiency. For today, I consciously choose to make up my mind and trust my ways and my direction upon your loving responsibility. Help me to think less about what I think is best and more about what you have planned. I turn over my life to you and ask for your guidance alone. May your power be at work within me today for I am weak, but you are strong. In Jesus' name, amen.

Written many years ago now, and prayed many mornings, these words remind me of the right-sized responsibility I have in this life and in my marriage. They speak of God's greatness in my weakness. Ugh ... *weakness.* I have a hard time swallowing that still, sometimes, and it can bring me to my knees in humility. I have come to understand, as Kevin and I have been putting together the pieces of our brokenness, that we must find strength and courage to face three important facets of life:

Trials. I can say with certainty and honesty that we will all face trials. John 16:33 reads, *"I have told you all this so that you may have peace in me. Here on earth, you will have many trials and sorrows. But take heart because I have overcome the world."* There are many different trials and sorrows we can face in a lifetime, and, in my case, there were times when I wanted to bargain my way out of them. I didn't want to face the trial in front of me. Honestly, who would choose to face any trial or sorrow, especially at the magnitude they sometimes come? I don't take that lightly. We have friends whose marriages didn't make it after similar experiences. We have friends whose daughter was battling brain cancer for the third time and is still beating all odds, but all the while they bear the burden the disease and all that comes with it brings. We have friends who lost a five-year-old daughter to brain cancer within months. We have a friend who lost his wife and mom in a car accident on the way home from work. We have friends whose 18-year-old daughter was killed in an instant by an impaired driver. We have our daughter, who never should have had to go through four homes by the age of five. No matter their severity or length, trials will come, but we can have peace in the God who has overcome all. God sees each trial and weeps with us. He tends to places in our hearts that we didn't know could be tended to. He loves us dearly enough to refine us in fires we never thought we could walk through, and calms storms when they are raging.

That is the God I know: The God Who is the only reason Kevin and I are standing, though still striving, in a stronger marriage now. I don't say that just to have a Christian cliché response, but because I know now without a doubt that God will not waste one moment of any of your trials. He has walked before us and will go with us as we walk through other trials we have yet to face. With each trial, we have a choice in how we will respond. Will we stand at the threshold of Heaven and put our foot over that line to see what God may have for us, with hope for something different and an eternal perspective?

Transparency. Authentically letting others see my true self, with all the flaws, was, and still is, scary at times. But it has been a gift beyond measure. In my experience, hiding who God has designed me to be has resulted in fear and insecurity and prevented caring others from seeing and speaking into my life as God intended. My community of close friends, who have taken phone call after phone call, cried with me, prayed with me, led me back to gratitude, and helped me see things more clearly, wouldn't have been able to do so if I hadn't first let them in. Had I hidden from the recesses of my thoughts and feelings, I wouldn't be where I am now.

My kids have been amused (or, maybe, annoyed) by the different "feelings" charts around our house. We have colored versions, with faces to resemble expressions. We have lists of body sensations and emotions, categorized under three overarching feelings: *mad*, *sad*, and *glad*. We have even more detailed versions that have been laminated. (Yes, I have a laminator which is also used to preserve cherished pieces of art created by my kids. I'm a bit of a laminating nerd.)

When we acknowledge our deepest feelings and thoughts and bring them into the light, God can grow us, and the enemy has much less power to persuade us. Finding our significance and knowing our purpose in facing trials and being honest about them has been essential. Kevin and I have grown deeply, individually and as a couple, as we've chosen to take the steps into vulnerability and reaped the rewards. Sometimes that vulnerable place feels like a dark tunnel. It can leave you wondering if you will be there alone. But when we have the Lord and others to walk with us, it doesn't feel quite so scary. *"For where two or three gather together because they are mine, I am there among them," Matthew 18:20.*

Trust. It is foundational. An imperative. It is the core value of every human from the first developmental stage of life in infancy until death. But all of us have had trust broken in some way, some worse than others. In fact, loss of trust might be a child's first crisis, brought on by those who most need to provide safety and stability in one's early years of life, their parents. Erik Erikson, in his description of the stages of psychosocial development, states that "If the caregiver is reliable, consistent, and nurturing, the child will develop a sense of trust, believing that the world is safe and that people are dependable and affectionate. This sense of trust allows the child to feel secure even when threatened and extends into their other relationships, maintaining their sense of security amidst potential threats."[1]

In my experience, mostly secure trusting relationships were in place during my early years, but then, there was brokenness as I began to separate and gain my independence as a teen.

My sense of self-identity—I was at a natural age for individualization—began to fracture as I developed, but I knew how to trust foundationaly. Kevin, however, didn't have a strong base early on, and therefore, found it hard to stand firm and grow in trust later in life.

In those pivotal moments early in our relationship, when trust had to be built, it wasn't just about me trusting Kevin, it was about Kevin trusting me. About 15 years into our remarriage, 2019, we had a FaceTime call with a couple we had met in another state, and I will never forget the question the husband asked Kevin: "Do you trust Shawna?" Kevin quickly answered, "Yes," but he didn't seem convinced. The other end of the line was quiet for a while, and the gentlemen questioned Kevin again, "Do you trust Shawna? Do you really trust Shawna has your best interest at heart? Do you trust that she is really *for* you?" Kevin hesitated and then answered honestly, "No, I don't fully trust her." Can you imagine the look on my face after all I had been through, still standing by this man? I could have burst into tears, but I held them back with a tough, wide-eyed, distressed look on my face. If it wasn't for the other couple, I am sure something would have gone flying out of my mouth at that moment, but instead, I sat there stunned. I just could not believe he didn't trust me. As painful as it was then, Kevin's responses to me indicated he really didn't fully trust me. Impacted by his fractured early childhood attachment, feeling invisible in plain sight, and his lack of ability to fully trust God, himself, or anyone else in his life before, this need for trust prompted his next steps on his journey of learning. I demonstrated continually that I was still with him and fighting for him often, and I cared deeply for him even when I was upset or sad about our circumstances.

Our story, then, is one of trust broken by him and then rebuilt. One hundred cycles of breaking and rebuilding might be an exaggeration, but it feels accurate. The key is that trust *was* rebuilt. The capacity of the brain to rebuild blows me away. It has the ability to rewire and reconstruct that which has been lost. The capacity to trust or trust again is never completely forgotten. That said, trust can be broken in a moment, but takes far more time to rebuild, especially in cases of infidelity. The question becomes, "*Who* do we choose to trust?" We will always trust something. Is it ourselves only because someone or something has proved untrustworthy? Is it something that won't last? Is it inevitably the wrong someone because we honestly don't know where to put our trust? Or is it trusting ultimately in the One Being who will never change, and is our foundation? Our God who knows all and has provided us free will and, in His grace and patience, allows us our own journey of trust?

When we build a relationship with the One Who is always trustworthy, we find that we can build or rebuild anything. That has been the victory that resonates the most for us both. Even through all the rubble of our broken trust, Kevin and I have *chosen* to do our best to trust in God first. That allows us to work to rebuild the trust that God intended for our marriage.

"Though they stumble, they will not fall, for the Lord holds them by the hand," Psalm 37:24.

CHAPTER 25

That Friday, Mid October

I believe I was led to write my story to gain more healing and strength within, so I could share it with others in a professional manner. To truly see on paper what God had led me through, time and time again, brought me the confidence I needed to do this work. After writing the preceding chapters, I had a strong sense in my spirit from the Lord that this story wasn't finished. It wasn't ready to be put into anything formal, like a published book, yet the flow of words I had previously received abruptly stopped. I didn't know if God would have me start writing again.

Eventually, I felt led to start once more, but in the Spring of 2022, things became a little rocky again. We'd make progress, fall back, and make progress again. Then, we had a few rough conversations—one while we were away together celebrating our 50th birthdays. Why, after all the work we'd done, were we back to those now all-too-familiar arguments, followed by downward spirals that became so much bigger than they ever needed to be?

We decided together that individual counseling was our next step: I needed to determine why the deeper distress was rising relationally for me. Kevin needed to know what had his old defensiveness, lack of attunement, and lack of regulation on the rise. Feeling defeated, we cried out to God to help us determine what was next for us. We wanted to be in our marriage and also feel well. Yet, the relational pain was, sometimes, too hard to bear, preventing a longer stretch of improvement. The sorrow and grief were unique for each of us because our trauma themes, experiences and brain wiring were oh, so different.

I found yet another phenomenal therapist about an hour away to do some additional trauma therapy work using IFS (Internal Family Systems[1]), BSP (Brainspotting[2], EMDR, and SE (Somatic Experiencing[3]. After almost five years since I had been to counseling, I welcomed therapy work, knowing there was a reward for the effort. She and I built rapport and began deep work quickly. When I first came to her, I was in a state of confusion and remembered sharing with her that I wasn't sure what else might be going on in my marriage. Although we spent most of our time focusing on my trauma healing, we began to consider what Kevin might have been experiencing. She and Kevin's therapist had a collaboration call to discuss professional perspectives.

In addition to therapy, I knew I needed some quiet spaces to meet with God. I had always found beautiful times with God in the mountains and at the creeks, so I committed to do just that. One full day a month, I was going to drive to the mountains to be with God. It was time that was set aside just for Him and me, and it was there that my story was met by God in a powerful way that took me to places I could not have imagined on my own.

One beautiful Fall day in September of 2022, I took a drive without a map to what we in Arizona call the White Mountains.

It was a short drive through the windy desert roads. I found tall pines and a creek. It wasn't fancy, but it was peaceful and serene. Though there was a campground nearby, few people were there. But I did see some beautiful, deep red, long-haired, wild cows that are quite rare in our part of the country. They were close enough to touch.

As I sat with God, I remember first talking to Him about a prayer I had written days before.

> *"I lament Lord. This life, this marriage, this relationship can be hard. Yet mine with You is sweet. It is tranquil. I adore my time with You, yet when I am emotionally heightened, I lose that time. Your imagery, Lord, is significant to me. When I'm at home, I can walk to the lake near our house. Some mornings and evenings, it's beautiful. The reflection is something worth a picture. On other days it's too hot and unimportant to visit. That lake represents my marriage. The water isn't clear. It doesn't flow. And it is often grimy. There is algae from the bottom that somehow can't clear itself. It just rises to the surface, and nobody has been able to clear it up. It just seems to move around. Debris gets stuck in it. Old cans, fishing line, small things, big things. That algae is persistent. It finds a way to remain."*

That lake had algae that could come and go for years. Sometimes it seems to be better and then, it gets worse again. I knew that the word "picture" was representing something unique for this next season of life, so, sitting with God next to the creek after reading the prayer, I recorded the following words to remind myself of what happened, when no one was close and no one else could witness the miraculous. I had no idea how intimate this would be to me.

Oh, how significant our God is. As I was up at Christopher Creek in those Arizona mountains, I was praying in stillness. Journaling. Reading God's Word. The worship song playing in the background of my heart had the lyrics from a song titled, Firm Foundation.[4] I was thinking of the imagery of the lake that God had been giving me many weeks prior, realizing that is not the marriage that I want. The water was never clear and I could see someone continually getting stuck in the algae—the stuck one is me; the algae are Kevin's struggles. I wrestled with not wanting marriage if that is what marriage is. Not pretending the lake was so beautiful and yet the wind just blew things around. And as I was sitting there watching the algae in the creek, I realized it was different. I could see clearly what God was leading me to. The thought of making a declaration for the marriage I would stay for, not even particularly my current marriage, but taking a wider-lensed view of marriage and what the Lord would call marriage to be. As I spoke these words out loud, something profound happened. I was expectant of something that day; little did I know what it was. Talking to God in a soft voice, I recorded this in my voice memo: "Marriage is a refinement. It's the most refining, hard tool to clear off our algae. Maybe that's why you're here to show us that, God. I don't want the marriage of the lake. I don't want the marriage even if I get beautiful sunrises and sunsets. I don't choose to stay in that marriage. No. The moment Kevin is unwilling or uneager to do that work, I'm done. Hold me to that, God. If he's unwilling to do that work, to clear up the algae, to have living water, flowing water like a creek, I will go!"

As I spoke those words audibly, something shifted. I felt it and I knew it. I smiled to myself with a chuckle toward Heaven. As the wind blew, leaves fell on me. His Spirit was present; it was so evident. Chills rushed over my body. It was as if God Himself breathed agreement with me, a moment in my story I will truly cherish. He saw me and cherished me deeply. He was good with where my heart, mind, and soul were leading.

I felt the confirmation and knew God and I were secure with this plan. I hadn't always felt this sense of the Lord through His Spirit, but I could recognize it now. I didn't want to leave the rock I was sitting on that day. I would have been content to stay a while longer, but it was time to go home. When I arrived, I spent time writing what I felt pressed on my heart, and I shared it with Kevin to give him a sense of where I stood:

A Marriage I Will Stay For: One that has consistent growth and flowing water (creek analogy). Shows evidence of efforts to remove the algae (deficiencies, struggles, etc.). Has life, laughter, fun, spontaneity, curiosity, pursuit, playfulness, passion, care, and concern. Has room to dream & expand.

A Marriage I Will Not Stay For: One that has stagnant water, with algae consistently on the surface simply moving from one area to another (lake analogy). Shows little effort toward growth, or growth has come to stop. Has constant rupture without repair, strife without concern, little communication, or pursuit.

It was clear, and there was nothing to "read between the lines." Kevin received this well, and I had peace. As we moved through the next few months, I felt confirmation as I observed each of our choices in the relationship. Things were progressing well until one Friday, in mid-October. That morning, we were revisiting some volatile discussions and interactions that had begun a few days prior and, once again, had left us in distress individually and as a couple. Things had been said by both of us that touched our deep wounds. That we continued to do so still baffled me because I know we love each other, but in those moments, it's as if neither of us can see the other as an ally. These sad interactions had occurred far too many times to count.

That Friday, a month after my first visit, it was my day to go to the mountains again. I was certain I had shared that with Kevin and made plans to take his car (which was electric, so I had to plan ahead). But when that morning came, we were off on our communication. That was not unusual for us, yet this time, it was different—very different. He denied knowing I was going away for the day, got very agitated, and said I'd never told him. After a heated exchange for a couple of minutes, I called our code word, "monkey barrels," which meant we were to have a time out of sorts. We had an agreement that, when I noticed his dysregulation without an attempt to come down emotionally, I was to call the code word. Kevin was to come back from time out to our conversation calmly and make an attempt at a repair. We had done this dozens and dozens of times before. But this time, neither one of us had adequate words to share.

Kevin says he doesn't remember much of what happened. He

didn't focus on the code-word plan. Instead, he called me a few short minutes after I left and said it was just too much, and he was calling for a 30-day, *out-of-house* separation—one for which we had never created plans or even considered in our time together. He packed up and left as I continued my drive to the mountains in complete distress. He left the house in a bit of disarray, and I had no choice. He was moving forward and renting a room at an Airbnb. He felt at the time it was the best option to stop the destructive cycle, not cause me any more pain, and hold what he said were the boundaries I had set. The truth is, I had set boundaries, just a month earlier, based on the marriage I would stay for, but they were my boundaries, not his. His decision that day didn't align with them anyway. It was not okay. We had an agreement, and he knew my pain. I always thought he would hold true to his word and not harm me in this way. It was devastating.

Feeling choice-less, I was thrown back traumatically to the day, two decades prior, he had left me and our first marriage, and left me vulnerable in the matter. My body felt like it was happening again. There was sheer panic and terror consuming my nervous system. I pulled off the freeway into a hospital parking lot and made a call to a dear friend. I even thought for a bit about going into the ER that morning because I was nearly hyperventilating. It was awful. Again. My world felt like it had been turned upside down, and there was nothing I could do about it. I felt truly powerless. Desperate in the wake of the abrupt loss, I raged at the sheer injustice of it all, and I feared what it would look like to my sweet, innocent children.

I managed to calm myself and muster up the courage to drive out of that hospital parking lot and on to the base of the mountain. I knew I wasn't in any position to drive very far, and, in fact, I think I drove in circles for a while. Some memories from that day are still vague. But I do remember the many hours of phone calls to safe people in my betrayal trauma world, those who understood firsthand. I sent lots of prayers and petitions to God as well. My heart was grieved and sad while my mind felt the all-too-familiar fog and numbness. There was so much to contemplate and try to understand that day. Kevin's behavior got worse as the day went on. We didn't talk, but the texts were miles long. In some instances, he indicated that he didn't want to cause me more pain because he couldn't meet my needs, but in others, he blamed me. It was so confusing.

My son couldn't figure out why I was halfway up the mountain all day, but the other kids didn't clue in at all. If they had seen my swollen eyes or defeated body language, they would have known. Nothing was right, but I needed to pretend all was right because I had no idea what to share with them yet.

So, I mustered enough exterior calm to pretend for until bedtime. But that evening, I only got about three hours of sleep, while I was tormented by the torturer of our soul. It was quite honestly one of the darkest nights I had experienced in my life. I woke many times with images of darkness and a heavy fog all around me that felt like it weighed a thousand pounds. I would shake my head and try to make it go away but not much helped. I wondered where God was. I wondered if He saw me and why He was allowing this again! I had music playing under my pillow, and I held my Bible in my arms, but I wasn't able to read a word. I didn't want a divorce. I didn't even want a separation. I couldn't go through that same cycle anymore! I wrestled to hear God and to know what He had for me next. I pleaded for a sense that He was there. I tried my best to listen, and yet, where God should have been, I confronted a void.

⁓

The next morning, I did the necessary things with the kids and took a late morning nap. I was not a napper most days, and after a short time, I was awakened by what seemed like God sharing with me a possible new way to have peace and calm in our home *and* stay married. After a few minutes, I knew it was the Spirit of God. He shared with me a plan that wasn't the intimate marriage we had been striving for, but it wasn't divorce, either. In fact, it was like nothing either of us had ever thought about. It felt like God was giving me a third option—more of a platonic biblical marriage with honor and grace for one another. It was like He was helping us create a unique roadmap just for "us." It was an odd middle ground—what I would've labeled "married, yet separated," somewhere between the marriage I said I would stay for and a marriage in which I would not stay.

⁓

Kevin contacted me later that morning. He had also wrestled through the night and felt that the decision he had made wasn't the right direction. Although we were distant, emotionally, I was able to hear his words again, because I was no longer distracted by the potential implications of an out-of-house separation. I shared what I believed God had awakened in me after my nap, and he said that he'd had a similar experience. We agreed to talk at a coffee shop the next day: Sunday, October 16, 2022.

When we met, I was incredibly guarded at first. But he proved to be regretful about his runaway decision-making and began to apologize and acknowledge his errors and the harm he had done to me. We spent three hours at the coffee shop as he led us through what would become our third in-home separation plan.

At that point, we decided to tell the kids a bit about what was happening and what the long-term was likely going to look like. One by one, we told them about our likely future of being married yet separated. We both had worked so hard for so long to make this work, yet we wanted more than anything to have peace in our home, and for our kids not to be uprooted. We did a lot of things well together, but the communication and emotional connection were suffering greatly when we tried to grow closer. We considered leaning into something more—in a different sense of the word "more"—unique, individualized and out of the neurotypical boxes.

It was heartbreaking for us to share and heart-crushing for the kids to hear this news. Between them all, they had tears, prayers, and questions like, "Why can't you keep trying?" It was so difficult to walk through this with them. We desired that they knew the truth, but we didn't share everything. In fact, they knew nothing yet about that awful Friday before. That was for a later time when my heart could handle it.

After some more lengthy discussions and five days after he originally left (despite the loss on the prepaid Airbnb), he came home on what would have been the 25th anniversary of our first marriage. I decided that I did not want to be in our master bedroom. That was too painful for me as I grieved this new reality. I needed space to just be with God and have a place in the house that could be mine alone. So, I moved into what was my home office.

Because I work full-time as a coach for betrayed partners, I wanted the office space to stay professional and consciously separate, to give me much-needed time away from my personal story. It was a big enough room that a nice wood-shuttered partition converted half the space into my bedroom. Equipped with weighted blankets and a growing Scripture wall above my head as I slept, it became the place where the Lord did, indeed, tenderly meet with me. Now I had the areas I needed for my sleeping sanctuary and my office space, symbolically and tangibly separating the private and public parts of my life.

We spent countless hours, meanwhile, putting together our complete separation plan and how things would unfold. We prayed and sought the Lord as we put on paper how to keep this as consistent and clear as possible. We needed to know each other's expectations and know where to set boundaries. That insanely detailed document started at five single-spaced, typed pages. It was exhausting to write. In-house separations are tough, especially as everyone settles in. And it was the most formal of our agreements to date.

What a confusing time that was! It was important for us to seek clarity as we attempted to identify our needs, and the specifics of the agreement helped me honor my prior understanding of what kind of marriage I would stay for. One of the areas of our separation agreement that was so helpful for us was another visual analogy that provided a way to measure our level of connection and intimacy: picturing levels of marital commitment as bodies of water. It came from an idea conceived by a friend of mine. Kevin and I could relate to it, and hours stretched into days as we fleshed out what made sense to us:

The Puddle (0-25% capacity for connection): Shallow and Limited. Included: Polite hello's, acknowledging each other's presence in a room, kind small talk about happenings (i.e., weather, kids' activities, friends/neighbors, etc.), being able to interact together as part of the family. Logical but not emotional. Business-like transactions. No physical touch. No expressions of "I Love You." Separate sleeping arrangements.

The Pond (26-50% capacity for connection): Contained and Managed. Included: All of Puddle, plus basic acknowledgement of situations (i.e., "I know this is hard"), basic checking in (i.e., "How are you doing?"). Responses are kept to simple sharing of emotions (with limited conversation around them). Not focused on the other person or on restoration. Needs expressed by one to the other are limited to physical space, environment, etc., and basic acknowledgement and care for the other's emotions. Listening but not providing solutions. Repairs and amends provided when deemed appropriate by the individual. Appreciations and thankfulness shared. Some physical touch (occasional hug, hand on shoulders/leg). Limited expression of tenderness (babe, honey, sweetie). Separate sleeping arrangements.

The Lake (51-75% capacity for connection): Deeper but Boundaried. Included: All of Puddle and Pond, with deeper emotions shared. Scheduled check-ins. Longer discussions. Future around "usness." Requests for repair and restoration are shared with one another. More spontaneity in conversation. More time together. Dates with the intention of connecting and knowing one another. Increased physical touch (a kiss, hand holding, a warm hug). Possible sensual touch (e.g., a back rub). Deeper expression of love ("You are beautiful"). Shared sleeping arrangements.

The Ocean (76-100% capacity for connection): Vast, Deep, and Wide. Included: All of the previous levels at a greater frequency and intensity. Tell each other everything. Deepest sharing of our hearts. Empathy is expressed. Emotions, including sensual and sexual emotions (nothing is off limits). Dream together. Spontaneity. Safety. Fluid connection. Safe sharing of feelings, with each knowing the other is "for me." Shared sleeping arrangements. Sexual intimacy and connection. Physical touch and expressions of cherishment and adoration are limitless.

As we wrote it out, we decided that we could live with a large pond, and we would work toward that goal for the time being, cautiously taking it one step at a time. As we walked out this "new normal," adjusting our agreements and boundaries every 30 days, we found that we were following another unexpected path. Each week, things became a little more normal in our world, and though others may not have called it normal, it was, at least, peaceful for all of the family. The conflict had been reduced, and my grappling efforts to meet my deep desires could be set aside, at least for now.

CHAPTER 26

_____

A Major Puzzle Piece

During this, our third in-house separation, I knew that I needed to find space for myself to heal and adjust while I continued to offer betrayal trauma coaching support to clients. By God's grace, once again, I was able to make conscious efforts to put my personal story to the side while I helped clients navigate their own stories. It was actually a nice reprieve, and I was cognizant of the need to keep my client load lighter.

One evening in late October 2022, I decided to do some admin work before I wrapped up the day. As I was cleaning up some emails, I saw a podcast that had been sitting in my inbox for weeks. I had a client who had mentioned it was worth listening to, so I popped in my air pods and listened while I multitasked. It was a podcast from a therapist who specialized in sexual addiction, and something called _neurodiversity_. I had heard that word before but didn't have much context for it, so I was eager to hear what she had to say. Within ten minutes, I had slowed, and then stopped, what I was doing. "Oh my gosh," I thought. "This is my husband!"

The speaker was neurodiverse herself and was on the autism spectrum. I paid close attention to her words. Her description of her own lived experiences were shockingly parallel to many things Kevin had said and done before. Since Kevin and I weren't quite on deep-conversation terms, I wondered what I was to do with this information.

I had found some tranquility in the evenings by climbing into our outdoor hot tub to talk with God and just listen to what He had for me. That night I had a purpose and knew I wanted to ask what I was to do with the information from this podcast.

After some quiet time of listening, I came inside confident to share the information if it felt right. It felt like a moment to hold loosely and that there wasn't a right or wrong answer. It had been years since I offered Kevin a book to read or a podcast to view, because I had really worked hard to not over-function in our relationship. We were saying goodnight when Kevin mentioned that he was going to take the next day off work. He wanted to spend some time processing and praying in an attempt to get straight in his mind his next steps in his own therapy work. He was struggling with:

- why his capacity, or lack thereof, was causing so much heartache and pain.
- why he couldn't meet my emotional needs.
- why this seemed to be our final outcome for our marriage.
- why, all this time, it had felt like he was trying to fit a square peg into a round hole, regarding emotional connection in marriage.

Given that Kevin was taking the day off and that my motive, this time, was not to achieve a particular outcome, I took a brave step, and risked a response I'd heard from him many times before: "So you think you know what is wrong with me? Are you going into coach mode?" I feared he would think I was trying to pin another "label" on him, but I knew that wasn't the truth. The risk felt worth it because I wasn't expecting much in return except a cordial reply. I was pretty familiar with risk, so I took a deep breath and said, "Hey, I listened to a podcast. I heard some things that you may relate to if you want me to send it to you. You can take it or leave it. Whatever is best for you."

He replied, "Sure, you can send it." It wasn't an aggressive reply, but it wasn't warm and fuzzy either. More like nonchalant.

The next day he called, while running errands. I answered the phone, thinking it was something about logistics—picking up the kids, or asking if I needed something while he was out. He was no longer nonchalant: "I can't talk about it now, but I can share more tomorrow. I have been crying, and I am a wreck after spending the last four hours listening to that podcast, he said, adding significantly, "I feel so *seen*."

That podcast was about forty minutes long, but it had taken him four hours to listen to and digest it. I'd had no idea if he would even listen to it, so its impact on him was a surprise. Not surprising were the weeks he spent watching many more podcasts, and digging through medical white papers to find out all he could about the autism spectrum and the traits exhibited by those with a high degree of Asperger's Syndrome. With his clinical nursing background, it was his style to do all the research. He knew the reputable self-assessments and took them all. Autism offered some explanation for the "whys" in his life, and he'd never felt more known than he did when reading the pages written by those who studied it.

My current therapist was the only one who had ever asked me if autism could be a possibility that summer before. During the eight months I'd been meeting with her, there were times that she had mentioned the characteristics, and she'd remained curious about the possibility that Kevin could be autistic. In fact, three months into therapy with her, I had actually mentioned autism during a date with Kevin and asked him if he would consider taking a little self-quiz that I'd found on the internet. My score for him had indicated that autism was possible, but his score said it wasn't autism. I didn't know enough about it and certainly didn't want to *label* him without certainty. So, given his lack of curiosity about it, we dropped it.

The weeks that followed Kevin's viewing of the podcast were tricky. While we were talking about all things autistic, deconstructing societal perceptions, and understanding the possibilities inherent in being a neurodiverse couple, we were also preparing for the process that would confirm his claim that he had been faithful to me, physically and emotionally, during the previous thirteen years.

As we continued on these two paths, I did receive healing on one front. His behavior had been so erratic on that horrible Friday in October that my uncertainty, since then, about Kevin's marital fidelity had me in a tailspin. That he'd decided, unilaterally, to rent the Airbnb rather than separate in-house was a big concern, given his previous acting-out behaviors. I needed to know, with as much certainty as possible, that he had been faithful. Thankfully, I knew what that looked like. I had a good picture of how I could ask for what I needed, but unlike thirteen years prior, I wasn't going to do a DIY-style disclosure.

A favorite author and friend of mine put it this way: "Walking fully in the light means being 100 percent truthful with each other. Ninety-nine percent of the truth is still a lie. The truth cannot be filtered or watered down."[1] If he hadn't been faithful or if there were more lies, I always knew that would officially end our marriage. He knew that, too. It was a bottom-line boundary.

With help and support from our coaching guides, we decided to prepare for a formal full-disclosure by Kevin. He would offer it in written form, then verbally share any deceptive or hidden behaviors, and, finally, provide answers to my questions. Afterward, a fidelity polygraph would be administered by a specialized professional. This was to verify the truth in the most certain way established in the field of intimate betrayal and problematic sexual behavior.

As we moved into this process, I felt denial stronger than I ever had before. As I vetted the questions I would soon ask him about our years together, the possibility that I could have been fooled again gave way to intense anxiety for me. I wanted to pull my covers over my head and just plug my ears. I remember wanting to chant "la, la, la, la, la," as if I were a child refusing to listen to someone talk. Yet, I pushed through with the mercies of the Lord each day as He carried me! I had come too far and built more resilience than I had thought possible. I wouldn't choose denial consciously. These efforts were now underway in the background of all other reintegration plans.

About three weeks after Kevin returned home from the out-of-house separation he had imposed, we were trying, together, to gently bring back a simple check-in with one another and, as Kevin shared with me the possibilities of what could be, I sat in my newly established half-bedroom/half-office and cried. I gave myself permission to cry in front of Kevin as I had in years past, and on that day, I could not stop. The tears flowed for hours. It felt endless. I was in deep despair and sadness.

The week prior, I hadn't reached out to any my closest friends, but on that tearful day, two of them were talking, and due to the sweet whispers of the Holy Spirit, they realized that I needed extra care and love. They invited me to dinner that night to check on me, but I just wanted to stay home and cry. This wasn't like me. Most often, when I got a spontaneous chance to sneak away for a Sunday dinner out, I would grab it. Sadly, I felt like a burden this time. I was *so* done with talking about the stresses in my marriage with its merry-go-round attempts and failures. The spiritual warfare had me pretty wrapped up, so I almost didn't go. I was grateful that evening that Kevin encouraged me to go and just be with them, even if I didn't have anything to say. So, I went.

I got to the little Italian restaurant looking like I hadn't slept in weeks—an image a bit too close to my reality. The kid who served us kept awkwardly coming to the table to ask us about our order only to find me crying nearly every time. But my sweet friends knew I needed this time together. They knew I needed encouragement and to be reminded I would get through this, too. There was a moment when I said to them, "I feel like a burden and don't know what to share anymore." Then, there were three sets of tear-filled eyes, and they assured me they wouldn't be there if they didn't want to be. That settled my heart, and they reminded me of what I already knew: Seeing myself as a burden was not at all my normal response. And they lovingly pointed out that I sounded really low and that they hadn't seen me like that before. I was grateful that we have the kind of friendship where we can cry those ugly tears together, yet also call each other out when things seem off. I absolutely know that it is a gift and I cherish it.

There was another element of that conversation at the restaurant that brought me clarity as I awaited not only verification of Kevin's faithfulness via the polygraph but also, now, the likely confirmation of the autism diagnosis. I knew where I stood on the faithfulness discussion and what my boundaries were. I knew that divorce was an option, depending on how that turned out.

As for the autism diagnosis, I saw it as a last opportunity to save our marriage from the newly accepted "married and separated" status we had been working toward. If the diagnosis was not confirmed, however, there was no chance that we could successfully strive for the "ocean marriage" we had always longed for. I was truly out of routes at this point, and yet, I still believed God saw us and had some sort of plan.

The next day, I contacted my naturopathic doctor to request a low-dose antidepressant. I needed it, and though I knew of the side effects, I also knew it could be a temporary solution while I worked to regain my emotional homeostasis. I was taking various steps to heal, and this one was important for me, too. Unlike in previous years, I experienced no shame or embarrassment during this season of antidepressant use.

As we waited for the day of disclosure, his behavior throughout the process led me to believe that he was, in fact, telling the truth about his faithfulness. When the day came, Kevin had included all acting-out behaviors from before we met and answered all of my many questions. I felt uneasy and rattled inside as he read out each behavior, one by one, pulling my thera-putty hard enough to release my angry energy for his careless behaviors. And, with sighs of release, I realized that there was, thankfully, nothing new.

Two mornings later, Kevin flew out-of-state for the polygraph to verify the truth with my choice from among the top polygraphers in the nation. As he left the morning of the polygraph, I said, "Thank you for doing this." He replied tearfully, "You deserved this a long time ago. I am honored to do this." There was such a confounded breadth of complex emotions (for both of us) when he said that to me.

That afternoon, the results came back. He had passed the polygraph *without deception indicated.* My heart and mind rested at such a deep level at that moment: He had humbly chosen to verify the truth because he had recognized that his previous infidelity and dishonesty had fractured our trust and made a lasting impact on our relationship, especially with the recent and startling Airbnb stunt. *This* was the marriage I would stay for, even if we were still separated.

Now, back to the possible autism diagnosis.

Although I was now convinced that Kevin could be

identified on the autism spectrum, and the clinician he had visited reported that there was a very high probability we were right, Kevin is too clinical, by nature and by professional background, to go with self-diagnosis. We knew self-diagnosis is the option for many, and we didn't knock it. But we just knew it wouldn't provide him with sufficient validation. We were grateful that we had a good insurance plan at the time, and that he had found a specialist who understood adult autism. We quickly learned that working with a clinician who specializes with adults does make a difference, because there is less funding available for adult autism, and there is a greater likelihood that adults will camouflage their behaviors with those around them, making it harder to diagnose.

Our confidence in our choice of clinician was confirmed. The results of her assessment matched all the subcategories of the diagnosis that were consistent with sensation avoidance, obsessive-compulsive, aggression, narcissism traits, emotional avoidance, negativism, and a few others. The moment she announced, "I am going to be giving Kevin the diagnosis of ASD [autism spectrum disorder]," we already both knew, deep down, that it was coming.

The diagnosis left me speechless. And I am rarely speechless as you can probably imagine. My processing speed, when I am identifying my emotions, is pretty quick now, given all the practice. But not this time.

After holding himself together on the call, Kevin dropped his head into his hands and said, "I'm so sorry. I'm just so sorry. I didn't know. It could have looked so different." He wept. He was nearly beside himself in tears. That was rare, and I had only seen him cry a few times through the years. Neither one of us could quite believe we had been dealing with this for so long. This diagnosis hadn't come out of the blue. As I sat silent, unable to produce words, I was flashing back to our first argument; to his first marriage proposal, delivered when I had my head in the fridge; and to that first night I saw him with his friends. It all made sense, from the underlying emotional deprivation we earlier identified to the avoidance of, and difficulty establishing, connection.

After twenty-seven years, a reality that had lain just under the surface had suddenly been brought into clear view. This new revelation was hard for both of us. We each were grieving and processing the news in our own way. My heart hurt for him, and my heart hurt for me. His heart hurt for all my heartache.

For Kevin, it was a relief, in one sense. The official diagnosis was Autism, Level 1, formerly known as Asperger's Syndrome, the least severe of three levels of autism. It explained so much. But it was also sad. A neurodivergent man in a neurotypical world. He had worked hard to fit into a world that demands we be "normal", but he was "that gifted kid" who had a hard time making friends and figuring out social cues, who had to try harder because nothing came easy socially or emotionally, who pushed back and even rebelled, at times, to ensure that others did what they were supposed to, in hope that he'd be seen. Intelligent, yet viewed only as "different" in a world where he was told there is only one way of doing things, he had rarely been appreciated for who he truly was, so he'd learned to mask and camouflage. No surprise, then, that he might resort to dishonesty, withdrawal, or defensive behavior.

It was sad for me, too. Many times, when I had seen the avoidance of emotional intimacy present, I believed deep within it wasn't intentional. He was trying, but the capacity to connect with me often wasn't there. Adding to the confusion, that capacity wasn't consistently *absent* either. He couldn't simply admit that it was hard for him to relate socially and emotionally. Instead, he would blame me, saying it was because I had communicated something unacceptable, or done so in an unacceptable manner. He had used many maladaptive coping strategies to remove that "different" label.

But the diagnosis also provided some relief for me. We now knew that emotional reciprocity—the give and take of feelings typical in a close relationship—was a major deficit for him and always had been. I now knew that he really had tried to understand how I felt, but most of the time, he couldn't. Instead, he would just guess at it. And *that* had left me feeling that he was just checking off another box. He would offer to me a "pretend" version of emotional commitment that he couldn't sustain, and then, again and again, ask me to give him another chance. That was crazy-making for me.

I remember so vividly the day when he said, (actually yelled), "Why can't I be normal?" He had asked that question just days before I listened to the podcast that had changed everything. Looking back, I see there was nothing random about the timing. Normal was always the standard he was going after, and, in my ignorance, normal is what I was looking for from him, too. There was so much we didn't know and still needed to learn.

That was confusing for me. What practical impact would the diagnosis have on our life together? If "normal" was no longer Kevin's goal, what, if anything, would have to happen with the "married but separated" agreements and the new realities we had been moving toward?

For the next several months, we learned about what life could or would be like with the acceptance of neurodiversity in our marriage. We listened to many more podcasts and bought books and workbooks in an effort to better understand the nuances of Kevin's diagnosable characteristics.

In time, I welcomed this new reality, and I welcomed his unmasking. It almost felt like I was finding out who he was for the first time, and I think that was true for him, in some ways, too. We took the time we needed, and the days were long, mixed with a lot of disappointment and appreciation. We continued to pursue our "large pond" goal while living apart in the house.

We began to view his life—our lives—through a neurodivergent lens, but we took care not to neglect the old lenses of addiction recovery, intimacy avoidance, and grief. We needed all the lenses. We also realized that some things could not be changed because they were hard-wired into Kevin's brain. There were many times I would bring up metaphors like "water off a duck's back," and he would struggle to determine what I was saying. He'd say things like, "Where is the duck? Why are we talking about ducks now?" That is wiring that neither he nor I can change. However, we both knew that the brain is neuroplastic and can change in some ways. For example, though Kevin had a hard time recognizing and naming emotions, with practice and repetition, he was learning how to familiarize himself with those feelings. In fact, I think, the greatest gift, so far, is that Kevin has realized, for the first time in his life, that he doesn't have to be—or pretend to be—someone he is not. He had learned how to take off the masks behind which he'd hidden his addiction, and he'd let go of the unhealthy coping in relationships to find love. Now he could take off the masks in all other areas as well.

For my part, I had recently learned that many of Kevin's behaviors are not personal. Even though they weren't meant to hurt me, they greatly impacted me. Similarly, my responses or reactions in anger, disappointment, and despair weren't meant to hurt him. That said, we each have needs, and those needs are important. In our worst moments, when those needs go unfulfilled, we speak not to purposely hurt the other, but to express our own hurt in the hope that we will be heard. Our brains are different, but we now have more room to hear and understand one another. We will probably spend the rest of our lives working together with this new insight and information.

We are different, we are unique, and we are all okay. Each of us has broken parts, but we are not completely broken. We are made whole, and I am reminded of a Scripture that I hold dearly and still holds a special place on my bedroom's Scripture wall. During so many moments with Jesus, I had heard it resonating in my spirit yet had never known what He fully meant. Now I do. *"See, I am doing a new thing! Now it springs up; do you not perceive it? I am making a way in the wilderness and streams in the wasteland,"* Isaiah 43:19. He was doing a new thing all along. Waiting in the grief and the hope and the "not yet" has proved a powerful place to be.

Now our job is to humbly lean in.

CHAPTER 27

Putting the Parts Together

It's been a long journey, and the journey continues each day. We certainly don't have it all figured out. I still go to therapy as I need to, doing work at a deeper, *subcortical* level—the hot spot of the brain that fires when attachment is disrupted, old trauma wounds get hit, and the threat response system gets hijacked. Although I wish I could say the masking is gone and tenderhearted appreciations given and received in those first few months following Kevin's diagnosis had held strong. They did not. We each went in and out of our own survival modes many times and, truthfully, we still do. We know, and it has been confirmed by experts in the field, that "our brains do, indeed, make indelible memories of the traumatic events; events that, for some, continue to replay like old home movies, even after they tire of the scenes that run and rerun in the theater of their minds."[1]

I know God has sweet sentiments for the sacred therapy work I both love and hate, and there are days I don't want to make the hour drive to therapy, to cry, deplete my energy, and shift my perspectives once again. In some seasons, I just want simple, but I know myself. I know simple doesn't always equate to growth, and growth is what I long for.

———————

Internal Family Systems, Brainspotting, EMDR, and somatic work are, at this point in my life and my career, my absolute favorite modalities for bottom-up therapy. As this category's name suggests, bottom-up therapy refers to starting the healing process in the limbic system and subcortex, which are the seat of survival, belonging and emotions, as opposed to more familiar talk therapy approaches, which put the focus on the prefrontal cortex, the thinking brain. After several months of processing the outcome of the new diagnosis, discussing my decisions, setting boundaries, and finding stability and safety again, I was ready to really look at every part of me.

Internal Family Systems is a model of therapy that understands humans as having varied unique parts and a core Self, called the God Image or *Imago Dei* by faith communities. With specific thoughts, feelings, sensations and agendas, each part works uniquely and interdependently with other parts, or aspects of our personalities. We are all born with parts that have positive roles and start out unburdened. Through life and hard experiences, some parts become burdened with pain and begin to encourage us to cope in helpful or unhelpful ways.[2]

This quote sums up well how this ties into Scripture: "It's helpful to remember that major figures in Scripture describe an inner world of parts in conflict. Consider the Apostle Paul. He famously wrote: *"I do not understand what I do. For what I want to do I do not do, but what I hate, I do,"* Romans 7:15. Consider David. He shares his Battle of the Parts all through the Psalms. One day it's "I absolutely trust you God!" The next, it's, "I'm dying here! Where are you, God?" Then we have the Apostle James. He seems to point to the same dynamic when he asks, *"What causes fights and quarrels among you? Don't they come from your desires that battle within you?" James 4:1*[3]

<hr>

I have parts that are protective. Some are proactive, and some are reactive. I call two of my key proactive protectors the *problem-solver* and *the investigator*. The problem-solver is responsible—sometimes too responsible. It can step in, take over, assume control, and then over-function. Somatically, in my body, it's a pair of grabbing hands, as if to say, "Give it to me. I can handle this for you."

The investigator is logical and can sometimes forget that the body and heart have something to say. This part can get a little too head-heavy and shows up in intense thought. Its purpose is to make sense of things, seek evidence, and defer to others for answers. These proactive protectors, also known as *managers* in the IFS world, have some very important jobs but often get themselves too far into situations where their help really isn't necessary.

My investigator part tries to do some diligent work to take situations down a path that may or may not happen, playing out lots of scenarios and putting barriers in place in certain situations that, for me, arouse wonder and keep me curious.

Although these detective skills, honed in my earlier years, aren't needed all the time now, I sure do appreciate the role they still try to play to keep me safe and secure.

I also have *reactive* protector parts, also known as firefighters. I have tenderly named two of them *the guard* and *the fighter*. They often sit back and let the managers try to do their work first, but if the pain does not diminish, then they come to the rescue as a last resort. The guard shows up with eyes wide open, really alert. This part is hyper-vigilant and takes on the role of scanning environments, watching certain people closely, and making judgments about their intentions, motivations, and expectations. However, the guard is a really fast processor, sometimes faster than my conscious mind can even process, so there is the danger that it will make assumptions about the same, based on little to no evidence. But it sure tries hard and can team up with the fighter.

The fighter is usually the last protector on the scene, when all else has failed. The fighter shows up with fists out and can be pretty angry—imagine that 13-year-old teen who is strong, dominant, and aggressive. The fighter expresses my most shameful behaviors—self-promotion, pridefulness, and defensiveness—and frequently does so at high volume. That said, I am learning to embrace this part who has tried to helpfully take on a needed role at certain points in my life.

With all these protector parts, I am reminded that I can trust they were and are there for a reason. Instead of wishing them away, I am learning to bring them close and give them space and voice, having them blend with all other parts of me. They are there to protect the parts of my being that have been asked to hide, to go away, or not have a voice. These cast-out parts are what the IFS world calls *exiled* parts. I consider each one of these exiles "dear ones" now.

The following are my exiled parts, listed from youngest to oldest (referring to when I think they were most unseen):

- The vulnerable one, who feels powerless, stuck, and

enmeshed. This part often needs clarity and compassionate care.

- The sweet one, who is so tender, sensitive, and vulnerable. Several protectors like to come forward for this one because connection is what this part needs most.
- The alone one, who can feel unseen, left, abandoned, or lonely. This part needs companionship and understanding to be willing to move forward.
- The scared one, who shows up with self-doubt, confusion, uncertainty, and, ultimately, fear. This part seems a bit older and needs clarity and confidence.

I share them with you now as a part of my journey. With God, all parts of me are welcome, each filling a role in my life. I don't need to be afraid or ashamed of any of them, and I am also helping them learn that they don't need to take over. "When we have full access to our God Image, we will spontaneously (with no effort) experience ... the Eight Cs: curiosity, compassion, courage, connection, clarity, calm, confidence, and creativity."[4] When I do bottom-up therapy work and spend time with these parts, God heals the wounds and disputes the false beliefs of their past. I can see the shifts in my behavior, but I don't always know how and when these parts-in-healing will come into play until the next time. But I do know that there will be *many* next times. I am responsible for myself and must seek further healing, no matter what Kevin chooses to do. I do know that my desire remains to stay and grow in our relationship; that hasn't changed.

I know the need for there to be continued growth from Kevin. He has continued with therapy and learning from individual groups, but since the diagnosis, he has wavered a bit—

in and out of acceptance—and, at times, he's dropped the ball and caused me hurt. There was, for example, a workbook we acquired shortly after the diagnosis, one on which Kevin had said he would initiate a joint study effort. But it sat untouched on a bookcase that I walked past multiple times every day for more than five months. On most days, however, I can observe his continued acceptance of the way his brain is wired.

These are some of the things we've noticed in our marriage through the years that helped us see we needed to view our relationship through a neurodiverse lens:

- When communication continues to feel like you're speaking two different languages.
- When other professionals have given diagnoses that just don't seem to fit.
- When not just one but many or most areas of relating feel so different (social interactions, sensory sensitivities, processing speeds, intimacy needs, cognitive flexibilities, etc.)
- When you often feel disconnected, misunderstood, confused, unknown.
- When you are genuinely willing, open, and honest but still miss each other.
- When even solvable problems feel impossible to solve.

Each person on the autism spectrum is unique, which makes each neurodiverse relationship unique. The following is a list of specific characteristics we have personally seen in our marriage around autism or neurodiverse behaviors[5]:

Social Interactions: Having a hard time feeling included, keeping a record of what works/what doesn't and copying behaviors of others, feeling anxious when in unfamiliar groups, interrupting to keep up with conversations, and lack of a theory of mind (related to others' experiences).

Expressive Communication: Focused on details, linear and logical, delayed response time, monologuing versus dialoguing, seems rude or sharp, omission of context, reluctant to speak for fear of getting it wrong.

Receptive Communication: Missing tones, facial expressions, and nonverbal cues; sensitive to other's volume; literal interpretation; unique assumptions; frustration with misunderstanding; difficulty keeping up with the conversation when multiple people are talking; frustration when more than one question is asked at a time.

Obsessions and Repetition: Hyper-focus on hobbies, perfectionistic tendencies toward one's self and others; and perseveration on certain topics.

Cognitive Differences: Exceptionally long-term memory, rigid and inflexible thinking, lack of spontaneity, forgetting parts of conversations, weakened short-term memory, and weak central coherence (sees the trees but not the forest).

Intimacy and Emotional Connection: Lack of identification of feelings (alexithymia), limited emotional reciprocity (back-and-forth connection), overwhelmed by emotional closeness, difficulty trusting that others' intentions or motives are good.

Sensory Sensitivities: Hyper and hypo-sensitive to sound, touch, light, smell, and texture; overwhelmed with crying or shouting; and difficulties with clothing textures, materials and tags.

Developmental Delays: Struggle fitting in with same-age peers; appears naïve, vulnerable, and unable to stand up for self; under-functions in tasks and task initiation.

Executive Functioning: Trouble prioritizing, following through, and completing tasks; lack of awareness of consequences for negative decisions; categorizing and systematizing instead of doing the task itself.

Anxiety: Acts out of fear of doing something wrong, has a tough time facing multiple tasks, and is overwhelmed easily.

Additionally, to help support one another, we have taken the following into consideration in our marriage:

1. Without the neurodiverse lens, the neurotypical (NT) partner can feel alone and discouraged in searching for answers to the ongoing difficulties.

2. Without the neurodiverse lens, the neurodiverse (ND) partner can feel confused and ashamed for neither understanding nor having answers for what is causing the difficulties.

3. The internal and external worlds of both partners feel very different.

4. There can be strain and unnecessary frustrations when trying neurotypical methods of couples therapy without neurodiverse information and insight because the approaches are different.

5. Using a neurodiverse lens can bring compassion and understanding.

It was and continues to be important to us to know what we might need at each step into this new reality. Based on our experience, I encourage the following for couples:

- Consider the current care and treatment course. Is the timing right to consider the neurodiverse lens or an assessment?

- Don't narrow your focus completely. There are often layers in couple's recovery course work (e.g., addiction recovery, trauma work). These might still need to be a part of your work together. Don't throw one treatment course out to take another. See if the courses can converge.

- Determine realistic expectations. What can be done at this time, and what adjustments can be made? Is there one new thing to consider?

- Take it slow. As a NT partner, don't flood the ND partner. What is the most important element to consider now?

- Determine if a Neuropsychological Evaluation is important to either or both of you and consider self-assessments.

- Focus on what can be changed. If both are interested in engaging in the same work, work together. Yet, let the ND partner do most of the research and take the steps forward to gain a better understanding. If your partner is not open to working together, see what you can do for yourself.

- Keep your attention on self-regulation versus expecting the other person to regulate you. This work can take years, so don't lean on the other person, expecting them

to do for you what you can do for yourself.
- Make time for and look for opportunities to hear about the other's perspective and cognitive language. Listen to others: join support groups, talk to other couples and individuals who are in neurodiverse relationships.
- Offer compassion to yourself and keep it simple: one step at a time.
- Set a single intention, try a tool until you master that together.

CHAPTER 28

Still in Progress

Neurodiversity has had a lot to do with our relational struggles, from our first date until now. But we have learned that we cannot afford to focus our recovery work solely on neurodiversity or autism. That would lead us to a dangerously narrow trap.

Kevin and I were talking the other day, and I was reflecting on a reaction I had to his autistic trait of rigid and inflexible thinking that, when challenged by me, triggered behaviors from him of blaming and projecting. Although many of these behaviors are what got us into our destructive cycles, it would be a serious mistake to blame them all on autism. Instead, these cycles are traceable to trauma that likely long preceded my entry into his life.

Likewise, many of my reactive responses arise from my own trauma themes, which were there previously and then accelerated by his behaviors in my life. Someone's unhelpful reactions can include defensiveness, blame shifting, stonewalling (shutting someone out relationally without notice), criticism, sarcasm, gaslighting, withdrawal, emotional outbursts, and neglecting another (e.g., walking away). These and other abusive tendencies are behaviors that often help someone cope with underlying anxieties or uncertainty within themselves. These responses demonstrate a lack of capacity to self-regulate, and it is never appropriate to say they are autistic characteristics.

We both feel very strongly that the differences in brain wiring, and associated traits, need to be seen as distinct from destructive behaviors. They are not always easy to identify (and nearly impossible to spot in the moments of distress), but it is imperative that we do our work with someone who can help us see these differences from an outside perspective and help us identify the choreography that got us into our destructive dance. We are always learning and growing, persevering, and prevailing. This is, quite honestly, the hardest work I have done in this lifetime.

As I consider all that God has done in our marriage—all that He hasn't allowed, all that He has allowed, and all that we continue to strive for—I can look at things with greater insight. Each new process and perspective is like a new starting point. All of the healing and growth has taken a lot of time, but that time has not been lost. God has continued to share with us how to love first, how to lay down our self-understandings, how to apologize (we're still practicing), how to give and, especially, receive feedback openly, and how to choose a humble response.

After sharing with a close friend about writing this book, she said, "If we knew what this was all going to look like before it happened, we wouldn't have signed up for it." How true that is for me! It takes courage to fight for the right things, and it takes a degree of trust far beyond my capability.

A recent, Holy Spirit-led message from our pastor, drawn from Daniel 3:8-30, seems appropriate to share. Three Hebrew men, Shadrach, Meshach, and Abednego were thrown into a fiery furnace when they refused to bow down to the King, Nebuchadnezzar. The story has been told and retold in many church messages, but what I took away from this particular message was that the fire not only did not burn them but, by their faith, liberated them. It purified them and gave them a cause that overcame their fear. What if there is more to the fiery trials in our own lives? What if God has a purpose for our "fire" that transcends our pain? What if the Creator of the Universe gives us courage as we exit the fire, just like He gave Shadrach, Meshach, and Abednego, and sets us apart for greater things as we face the circumstances of our lives? What if Jesus is ushered into our fire with us, allowing us to see Him and follow Him more closely? Oh, the sweet fragrance of that fire, as it releases the goodness we might otherwise never know was possible in our lives!

I invite you to be with the God who knows much more than we do. We need not be defeated by our trials. This is a reminder I need to keep close to my heart as each day brings a little more clarity for the next, and I feel a greater sense of acceptance that the gap between my emotional needs and Kevin's capacities is wide in our relationship. Something God knew all along—though I even recently found myself upset at that reality—and finds great pleasure in our determination for more: more inspiration to take a step, more light for others to see, more legacy to pass on, more presence in reality, more thoughtful in consideration, more love to share.

I believe our story, thus far, has delivered more victories than defeats (depending on how you look at it and what day you ask me), yet maybe that's the way it's supposed to be. It has had its fair share of tragedy. I can attest to that. I try to see the hard days through the filter of Jesus, whose victory was won in agony. And I can't say for sure that I know where our marriage will end but we are believing it will be for good. For the glory will be for God and sacrifices for generations to come. And there is not a fairytale ending to this story. We're still in the middle. It is neither rosy nor perfectly buttoned up, but rather, real and messy.

I hope you have taken courage from that authenticity, as you've faced your own story. Many have shared with me through the years redemptive stories that preserved their marriages and maybe even found beauty beyond what they thought possible. Others have written about the victorious freedom of finding strength after divorce, each circumstance having its own brand of pain. For me—for us—I write in the in-between while it is not all figured out. But I'm not afraid of any story God may yet have for me.

Do you find yourself in a time when your spouse does not want to put in the work, accept his or her destructive behaviors, get a diagnosis, or even admit to their part in your marital struggles? There are times when God leads us to stop fighting for a marriage from which our spouse is in retreat. My personal encouragement, if this is you, is to take courage and keep fighting where He leads you, even if that's not for the relationship. It takes both of you. God can and will see that your work is not lost. I truly do know how it feels to have a spouse walk away and think that's the better route out of that broken place. I can assure you that it's exhausting and yet so very rewarding no matter the outcome when you've chosen to answer only to God, and in the quietness of your heart, know that you have done all you could do.

So, don't give up before the miracle. It might be a broken marriage in restoration, a shattered heart being rebuilt and healed beyond the marriage. It might be freedom from an abusive relationship, or it might be finding hope in a relationship that now looks so different than we've hoped. It might be a story God has never written before. But it's about staying the course we are called to. Let's listen to the voice of God together.

Through it all, I've come to know what being completely, utterly, wholly cherished looks like, and for that, I will be eternally grateful. I don't believe I would have known this kind of love and adoration from my Heavenly Father if our story had not unfolded as it did. His love—eternal, and full of meaning— overflows into a marriage covenant in which grief—even grief!—has eternal significance. Kevin and I have often said that this was not the story we would have written or remotely desired, yet because we have confidence that God permitted it, we will do our very best to use it for good. We will seek to honor where we are now.

With that, I conclude this book. It is a raw record of a quarter century of our marriage, but it is by no means the finished story. Our story is still in the making, one step, one challenge, one victory at a time. This, then, is in no way "The End." I leave you with this ....

God's not done with your story either!

ENDNOTES

Introduction
1. Shauna Shanks. A Fierce Love: One Woman's Courageous Journey to Save Her Marriage (Grand Rapids, MI: Zondervan, 2017).

PART I

Chapter 1
1. Referencing the distinction of pursuer and withdrawer from Dr. Sue Johnson. Sue Johnson, Hold Me Tight: Seven Conversations for a Lifetime of Love (Little, Brown Spark, 2008), 89-94.

Chapter 8
1. Oswald Chambers, My Utmost for His Highest. Edited by James Reimann (Grand Rapids, MI: Discovery House Publishers, 2005), June 8.

Chapter 9
1. Celestia G. Tracy, Mending the Soul Workbook (Phoenix, AZ: Global Hope Resources, 2009).
2. Tracy, Mending the Soul, 221-225.
3. Ibid., 206.

Chapter 10

1. Al-Anon Family Group Head Inc., Courage to Change: One Day at a Time in Al-Anon II (Virginia Beach, VA: Al-Anon Family Groups, 1992), 33.

2. Alcoholics Anonymous, "Into Action," in Alcoholics Anonymous: The Story of How Many Thousands of Men and Women Have Recovered from Alcoholism, 4th ed. (New York: Alcoholics Anonymous World Services, 2001), 84.

PART II

Chapter 11

1. Celebrate Recovery, 12 Steps, www.celebraterecovery.com.

2. Al-Anon Family Group Head Inc., Courage to Change: One Day at a Time in Al-Anon II (Virginia Beach, VA: Al-Anon Family Groups, 1992), 92.

3. Celebrate Recovery, 12 Steps, www.celebraterecovery.com.

4. "Welcome to COSA," International Service Organization of COSA, Inc., https://cosa-recovery.org.

5. Celebrate Recovery, 12 Steps, www.celebraterecovery.com.

6. ISO of COSA, "Working the COSA Steps," www.cosa-recovery.org.

7. Ibid.

8. What have come to be called the "9th Step Promises" is adapted from Alcoholics Anonymous, Alcoholics Anonymous: The Story of How Many Thousands of Men and Women Have Recovered from Alcoholism, 4th ed. (New York: Alcoholics Anonymous World

Services, 2001), 83-84.

9. Stephen Arterburn, and David Stoop. The Life Recovery Workbook: A Biblical Guide Through the Twelve Steps (Carol Stream, IL: Tyndale House, 2007), 909.

Chapter 12

1. For more information on EMDR, see https://www.emdria.org/ EMDR International Association. Austin, Texas

Chapter 13

1. Sheila Wray Gregoire, Rebecca Gregoire Lindenbach, and Joanna Swatsky, The Great Sex Rescue: The Lies You've Been Taught and How to Recover What God Intended (Ada, MI: Baker, 2021), 65.

2. "What are the Five Love Languages?," Love Languages, adapted from Gary Chapman, The 5 Love Languages: The Secret to Love that Lasts (Woodmere, NY: Northfield Publishing, 2015), accessed February 3, 2024, https://5lovelanguages.com/learn.

Chapter 14

1. Stephen Arterburn, and David Stoop. The Life Recovery Workbook: A Biblical Guide Through the Twelve Steps (Carol Stream, IL: Tyndale House, 2007), 1080.

2. Merriam-Webster, s.v. "trust," accessed January 23, 2004, https://www.merriam-webster.com/dictionary/trust.

Chapter 15

1. Kari Brooke Jobe, "I Am Not Alone" [lyrics]. Capitol Christian Music Group; songwriter: Kari Jobe; album: Majestic, 2014. https://www.lyrics.com/lyric/30636122/Kari+Jobe/I+Am+Not+Alone.
2. Sheri Keffer, Intimate Deception: Healing the Wounds of Sexual Betrayal. Ada, MI: Baker 2018), 289.
3. Sue Johnson, Hold Me Tight: Seven Conversations for a Lifetime of Love (New York: Little, Brown, 2008), 7.

Chapter 16

1. Susie Larson, Prevail: 365 Days of Enduring Strength from God's Word (Ada, MI: Baker, 2020), 224.

Chapter 18

1. APA Dictionary of Psychology, s.v. "detachment," American Psychological Association, https://dictionary.apa.org/detachment.
2. Al-Anon Family Group Head Inc., Courage to Change: One Day at a Time in Al-Anon II (Virginia Beach, VA: Al-Anon Family Groups, 1992), 42.
3. Lysa TerKeurst, Good Boundaries and Goodbyes: Loving Others Without Losing the Best of Who You Are (Nashville, TN: Thomas Nelson, 2022), 51.

Chapter 19

1. Dictonary.com, s.v. "obedience," accessed February 3. 2024, https://www.dictionary.com/browse/obedience.
2. Bessel A. Van der Kolk, The Body Keeps the Score: Brain, Mind, and Body in the Healing of Trauma (London, UK: Penguin Books, 2015), book summary

quote.

Chapter 20

1. Merriam-Webster, s.v. "sensual," accessed February 3, 2004, https://www.merriam-webster.com/dictionary/sensual.

2. Lawrence Richards, The Bible Reader's Companion: Your Guide to Every Chapter of the Bible. (Colorado Springs, CO: Chariot Victor, 1991), 748.

PART III

Chapter 22

1. For more information about The Association of Partners of Sex Addicts Trauma Specialist (APSATS) founded by Barbara Steffens, PhD, see https://www.apsats.org/ Dublin, Ohio.

Chapter 24

1. Saul Mcleod, "Erik Erikson's Stages of Psychosocial Development," Simplypsychology.org, updated January 25, 2024, accessed February 3, 2024, https://www.simplypsychology.org/erik-erikson.html.

Chapter 25

1. For more information on Internal Family Systems (IFS) founded by Richard Schwartz, see https://ifs-institute.com/ IFS Institute. Oak Park, Illinois

2. For more information about Brainspotting (BSP) founded by David Grand, PhD, see https://brainspotting.com/ Brainspotting Trainings, LLC.

3. For more information about Somatic Experiencing

(SE), see https://traumahealing.org/ Somatic Experiencing International. Broomfield, CO.

4. Cody Carnes, Chandler Moore, "Firm Foundation (He Won't)" [lyrics], songwriters: Cody Carnes, Chandler Moore, and Austin Davis, album: Firm Foundation (He Won't), Maverick City Music, 2022, https://essentialmusicpublishing.com/songs/firm-foundation-he-wont/.

Chapter 26

1. Rosie Makinney, Fight for Love: How to Take Your Marriage Back from Porn (Nashville, TN: B & H Books, 2020), 55.

Chapter 27

1. Barbara Steffens, and Marsha Means. Your Sexually Addicted Spouse: How Partners Can Cope and Heal. (Estes Park, CO: Armin Lear Press, 2021), 113.

2. Jenna Riemersma, Altogether You: Experiencing Personal and Spiritual Transformation with Internal Family Systems Therapy, ed. David Kopp (Marietta, GA: Pivotal Press, 2020), 18-19.

3. Riemersma, Altogether You, 5.

4. Ibid., 18.

5. "Neurology Matters in Couples Therapy: Training 101: Fundamentals of Working with Neurodiverse Couples in Therapy." Neurodiverse Couples Institute, Association For Autism And Neurodiversity (AANE). 2018, https://aane.org/services-programs/training-education/courses-for-professionals/training-101/.

ABOUT THE AUTHOR

Shawna Meek is a writer, an International Coaching Federation (ICF) Professional Certified Coach, a member of the board of directors as well as a coaching supervisor with the Association of Partners of Sex Addicts Trauma Specialists (APSATS), and the founder and owner of Living Stones Coaching, LLC. She began her work in the field of specialized coaching after finding strength through her own difficult journey in marriage.

Shawna has more than 15 years of educational, personal and professional experience and brings a unique and balanced perspective to her clients and supervisees. She currently reaches women around the world through her website, podcast appearances, group and individual coaching, and supervising other professionals.

Shawna is in a neurodiverse marriage to her husband, Kevin, and they have children ranging from elementary school age to married young adults. She has a strong faith in Jesus as her Savior, and knows that even through the darkest times, there is always hope for creating healthier relationships with herself and others. Shawna knows the courage and hard work it takes to heal after betrayal, and she has a passion to help others regain perspective, improve self-confidence, and make empowered choices.

- Website: www.livingstonescoaching.com
- Instagram: @livingstonescoaching
- Facebook: @livingstonescoaching
- Youtube: @livingstonescoaching9705

DEDICATION

To my husband, Kevin, who has courageously given me full permission to share our story and rallied me to keep writing when the days were long, and it was hard to recall our long, grueling story. To my precious kiddos who have been willing to share pieces of their story while cheering me on for this book endeavor and being so patient when I was writing for hours on end.

To my devoted editor, Casey, who from day one has been my cheerleader and doubt-buster in those difficult moments. To my second pair-of-eyes editor, Mike, who provided more than I thought I needed in this process. To my designers, Jenny and Jessica, who have been an incredible gift to design and layout the book in detail. To my book launch manager, Sarah, who helped me get the word out about this story. To my dedicated beta readers, prayer team, launch team and committed encouragers providing their valuable time believing in me and supporting me through the excitement and the tears.

And most importantly to the tender and gracious Lord, who not only gave me this wild idea but showed Himself present each step of the way.

RESOURCES

- Living Stones Coaching, Mentoring and Consulting. https://www.livingstonescoaching.com/ Gilbert, Arizona
- The Association of Partners of Sex Addicts Trauma Specialists. https://www.apsats.org/ Dublin, Ohio
- Hope Redefined Ministries. https://hoperedefined.org/ Knoxville, Tennessee
- EMDR International Association. https://www.emdria.org/ Austin, Texas
- Brainspotting Trainings, LLC. https://brainspotting.com/
- IFS Institute. https://ifs-institute.com/ Oak Park, Illinois (accessed websites March 1, 2024)

www.ingramcontent.com/pod-product-compliance
Lightning Source LLC
Chambersburg PA
CBHW020226130626
46549CB00005B/1761